praise for
gut check

"A modern day classic! Masterful!"

Catholic Men's Quarterly

"*Gut Check* is destined to become a classic!"

The Catholic League

"What a great read!"

Legatus Magazine

"Can't recommend highly enough!"

Catholic Exchange

"Gleeful camp likely to tickle anyone from Gen X, Y, or Z!"

Mercator.net

"A particularly worthwhile book for the modern guy!"

American Chesterton Society

gut check

2nd Edition

GUT
CHECK

Confronting Love, Work,
& Manhood

TAREK SAAB

RANSOM BOOKS • FORT WORTH
2008

Published in the United States by
Ransom Books
9280 Huntington Square
Fort Worth, Texas 76180

Library of Congress Control Number: 2007943492 (1st Edition)

ISBN 0-615-23061-X
978-0-615-23061-0

Printed in the United States of America

To my loving and patient wife, Kate

contents

author's note

MY INTENTION in writing this book is to reconstruct the decade of my life between the ages of eighteen and twenty-eight, to share and reflect upon particular events that shaped my growth into manhood. My account is part fiction—in a sense—to protect the people represented in my anecdotes. The events I mention are more or less accurate, but for brevity's sake, in some cases I have merged two events into one, or two people into one person. I may repeat a conversation from memory more or less exactly as it took place, or I may combine two or three similar conversations. I have set out to paint the most accurate picture of my bachelorhood in a condensed and creative manner.

"All men have an instinct for conflict:
at least, all healthy men."

HILAIRE BELLOC

gut check

2nd Edition

prologue

you're fired!

"TAREK—*YOU'RE FIRED!*" snapped Donald Trump, as he glared at me from across the boardroom table, in his dark blue suit, solid pink tie, and infamous hairdo. The ever-popular catchphrase from *The Apprentice*, lobbed at me by the real estate tycoon himself, on national television before a viewing audience of ten million, appeared in that particular instant to ooze from his mouth in baritone-pitched slow motion. Like the exchange of wedding vows or the verdict from a jury, the words presented an unmistakable finality.

As I sat, rigid and utterly exhausted, I paused to reflect on the circumstances that had landed me in that surreal place. I remember thinking how unimaginable it was that fate had brought me to this international stage. Surrounded by cameras and surrounded by fame, it was as though I had departed for a brief time from the world of ordinary life and entered into the fantasyland of dreamers. In years past, I had always possessed a naïve curiosity about Hollywood and the world of tabloids and autographs. As

3

The Donald was about to expel me from that universe, I realized that I was not playing a role. Rather, the character was *I*, placed on a platform for all to examine and evaluate. The culmination of who I had become, neatly packaged in a fine shirt and business suit, lay exposed as a vulnerable overachiever sensationally discouraged by Trump's stinging words.

Of the eighteen original contestants, seventeen were fired, and the intensity of the drama fluctuated considerably depending on each candidate's disposition. It is widely known that, through editing, a reality-TV personality is at the mercy of drama-loving producers. Yet without exception one's overall qualifications are still auctioned within the hearts and minds of the viewing audience. Since acceptance and validation are natural human yearnings, this national stage can be emotionally devastating to some and artificially glorifying to others.

Ten weeks into the fifteen-week process—May 1, 2006—I had reached the end of my run. Yet as the words shot from across the table, I was somewhat relieved. I thought Trump's words should sting more, but instead they echoed anticlimactically through the boardroom. Perhaps I can't claim total imperviousness, but in truth, it felt largely as though my firing was little more than a firecracker in my battle for happiness. I was protected by the very quality that landed me on the show in the first place, a state of mind that had grown organically through the droughts and floods of my twenties.

It was a state of mind characterized by *detachment*. There are many "experts" who preach a doctrine of happiness through "having it all." My experience was entirely the opposite. After tasting the bitter fortune of getting everything I had ever wanted, I realized that having it all was more of an anchor than a sail. My journey began in the winter of 1997.

part one

dead man walking

SUCCESS IN LIFE AND BUSINESS begins by focusing on *death*. Unfortunately, no one ever explained this to me in high school or in college, and Lord knows I never read it on the business rack at Barnes and Noble. Perhaps the truth is too morbid for your average business tycoon. The glaring irony of professional success is that, mortally speaking, the greatest leader ends up with the same fate as the guy with no initiative at all. The Grim Reaper is a communist, not a capitalist. He comes for everyone equally. In fact, I spent ten years of my life so preoccupied with Natty Light, girls, and the corporate climb up Mt. Olympus, that I totally missed the moral of this crazy human drama. But let me start at the beginning, somewhere in the middle of my freshman year in college.

Late one Saturday afternoon, as I slowly crept towards consciousness, I could feel an assortment of aches and pains shooting from my head to my legs, beginning with a throbbing migraine and its steady, unforgiving drumbeat. I had inhaled a Papa John's pizza at 4:30 AM, and the mixture of cheese and beer left my stomach pleading for Pepto. As I tried to swallow, a vile stickiness filled my throat, and I manipulated my face and mouth in an attempt to expel the nastiness. In the process, I turned my neck suddenly and felt a shooting stab down my spine, which I presumed was a gift from the $25 Salvation Army couch. The journey to the bed the night before seemed as enticing as Andy Dufresne's five-hundred-yard sewage crawl out of Shawshank, so I posted up on the love seat, summoning the memory of all the people who had undoubtedly violated it in years past. As I gradually began to lift myself up, I noticed my kneecap was missing a few layers of skin. Nice. In younger days, it would have been the type of thing that mom would have treated with a band-aid and a cookie, but left untouched it had grafted itself onto my Dockers—and no cookie. I couldn't remember why there were grass stains on my shoulder, but I was certain that it was a tragic laundry accident waiting to happen.

Not two minutes had elapsed before my roommate fired up *Madden '97*. He never had to ask for a game. There was always an unspoken duty to drop everything to assist a buddy in need when he had to get his *Madden* fix. It was the honorable thing to do. Besides, I shared a similar impulse. It was a picturesque day outside, which always inspired football.

"I'm hurtin."

"Yeah, me too."   ·

Aside from the requisite trash talking, we remained relatively speechless. We were saving our war stories, waiting for the rest of our crew to wake up before the formal recaps. Eventually our buddy Tommy (a Chris Farley look-alike and act-alike whose real name was Victor) rolled into the pad and alerted us to the fact that the room was probably a little pungent.

"It smells like somebody died in here."

"It's Bobby," I clarified, referring to my roommate, an English major with limited career aspirations.

"Let's go, it's time for breakfast," announced Tommy, making light of the fact that it was 5:00 PM.

"Save the women and children. Tommy's hungry."

"Lay off me, I'm sta-a-arving!"

Tommy had adopted a Chris Farley persona by this point, five months into our freshmen year, and he had him nailed. He was a goon, but a very likeable goon. I always wondered if the constant flood of self-deprecating jokes ever affected him. I couldn't imagine what he'd be like out of college fathering a family or managing people. Perhaps that's why they have reunions, just to satisfy the curiosity.

Though most of us lived within a two-hour drive of home, we rarely left campus. Our friends became our adopted family within this college utopia, and our first foray into adulthood was a surprisingly easy transition. Janitors cleaned our mess, cooks prepared our food, and our parents (or the student loan gods) covered our bills. If we held a campus job, it was by no means difficult, exemplified by my less-than-arduous two-year stint as the women's soccer manager. As if to magnify the situation, we spent less time in class than ever before in the twelve years prior. We idled amidst a lack of responsibility, and we relished it.

Our dorm sat proudly at the top of a very steep hill, and the long walk to the Caf was always better going than coming back, especially in winter. We hung in a large posse (about ten deep), and regardless of the day or the circumstances, we habitually ate at 5:30 PM every night. I doubt that anyone would ever admit it, but there was a comfort about it. We would overtake a specific table, and for the most part, stick to a set menu of cereal and side dishes unless one of us summoned the courage to try the day's special. The only variation was the seating arrangement, as everyone fought for the "offensive" side of the table. The "defensive" side placed your back to the Caf entrance, which made it difficult to scope out girls.

The dinner conversations were a mixed bag, but the bag never included anything resembling higher academia. We devoted much of our time into analyzing, dissecting, and ranking the female talent pool. We categorized the best looking as "The Dream Team": Lunchroom Goddess; Judy the Beauty; Dream Weaver; Melanie the Felony (who was still not quite eighteen); The Cookie Monster (who always got up to get a cookie for dessert but somehow never put on the freshmen fifteen). Some were less clever, like "Orange Cardigan Girl," who just happened to be wearing an orange cardigan the first time we saw her. We all had our favorites. Tommy would, without fail, contribute a husky Wisconsinite who he thought had "nice eyes," and we'd pepper him with obscenities and whatever crusty food was left drying on our trays.

Sometimes we'd get into heated debates about whether the '86 Celtics would have taken the '97 Bulls in a best of seven (is there any doubt?), or whether He-man was gay (pink shirt, cat lover), or who had the better 'stache: Tom Selleck or Geraldo Rivera (you gotta go Magnum P.I.). But one thing was a given: we'd always recap the war stories after a big night.

"I drank fawhteen bairs last night," boasted our buddy John Flanagan, getting us "stahtid" in his heavy Boston accent that he emphasized for dramatic effect.

Flanagan was the stereotypical Irish kid from Boston, and though our New Hampshire-based school was crowded with Irish boys, none of them were quite as over the top as Johnny. He reveled in his "Irishness," from his tricolor tattoo to his patchwork Irish cap. Naturally, he drank copious amounts of alcohol, and he didn't exaggerate about the fourteen beers. We had gone "high brow" with our investment of High Life bottles, and we saved the cap of every empty bottle in order to preserve an accurate count.

"You want a medal Johnny? I started, like, two hours later than you and still drank you under," big Tommy proudly asserted.

"Tommy, you weigh like 400 pounds. There's gotta be a slidin' scale. Actually, I'm sorry, I fuhgot you don't know what a scale is," Johnny replied, minus the gratuitous F-bombs. The fat jokes never got old, but Tommy seemed oblivious to it.

"Dude, what about lover-boy Bobby? Saw you makin' out with that blonde chick. Did you take her home?" asked my buddy Chris, changing the subject. He knew the answer was "no" before he asked the question, but it didn't matter. Chris steered every conversation towards sex. I'll spare you the sordid details, but we all had a good laugh about how Bobby got the Heisman from a girl that everyone agreed had chronic halitosis.

Chris had an obsession with porn. Computer porn. Porn magazines. Porn videos. He was proud of it, too. He was a big guy, great athlete, worked out all the time, and seemed older than everyone else even though we were all freshmen. Every group like ours had a guy like Chris. For some reason, he was the only one in our crew without a nickname. He had a presence about him. Everyone followed his lead because, like a big brother, he made us feel invincible, though most of us felt a little uncomfortable at first with the endless barrage of sex talk. The truth was, we were mostly conservative guys from good families at a small Catholic college. We weren't always morally upstanding, but we weren't exactly hedonists either.

"T-Saab. What about you, brother? Saw you chattin' it up with Secretariat," asked Ted McFadden, a.k.a. Mickey, a skinny kid obsessed with weed and rap music, but who would need to wait a couple more years before Eminem arrived on the scene and legitimized it for white boys. He was referring to the large nose of a girl named Jennifer.

"T, don't tell me you hooked up with that chick with the big muzzle!" added Tommy, who in actuality would have given his right arm to make out with anyone, but instead played along with Mickey.

"Nah, she's just some chick in one of my classes." I lied to save face. I had been very drunk, and all I could think about the night before was fooling around with her.

"Didn't look that way," egged on Bobby.

"She couldn't fight the fever, but I just wasn't feelin' it."

"I heard she gets taken five-hole more than our goalie," added Chris, referring to the fact that she was known to get around.

"Not last night. Saab couldn't seal the deal," slammed Bobby. In the span of one minute, the conversation had spun one hundred and eighty degrees. It always happened that way. Damned if you did, damned if you didn't. In this case, I hadn't. I explained how I had thrown up on the way out of the party and stumbled back to the crib, which earned the unified "attaboy" of the group.

"Yo, Orange Cah-digan Girl dropped by last night, T-Saab. Did you see her? I wondah how she felt about you and Schnoz." Johnny wasn't done with the goading.

In the pantheon of women on campus, I had Orange Cardigan Girl ranked Numero Uno. (No one had her ranked below fourth except for Chris, who claimed he could never date a girl with a small chest). He'd reminded me that on the way out of the party, it was OCG and her friend Molly who had assisted me in my regurgitating glory. In an instant my feelings descended from a little under the weather to flat-out depressed. I zoned out the rest of the conversation as they introduced a myriad of absurd anecdotes from the night before, from Jimmy D's near arrest for public drunkenness to Scooter's Zulu run (buck naked) through the women's dormitory at 3:00 AM. Tales like these became a red badge of courage for each of us.

Despite the stories, maybe even because of them, I desperately wished to erase the fun I'd had the night before. I had waited all year to meet OCG, and the climactic introduction was simultaneously fitting and tragic. There were girls on campus that we'd lust after in a purely sexual way, the ones who wore the skimpy fitted tops and tight jeans, pining for approval from guys but not realizing how badly we objectified them. Then there were the girls who'd melt you. In them you could see a reflection of your unworthiness, which introduced a level of self-awareness that went missing amidst your buddies. These women personified classiness through their speech, by their demeanor, and in the way they dressed, and their unassuming charisma enveloped you. It was easy to absolve them of any imperfections in the same way we did our mothers. To some extent we were even guilty of deifying them, as though they alone withheld the secret to our happiness. We fantasized about rescuing them in dark alleys, and though we may not have realized it, we had an innate desire to protect them. Orange Cardigan Girl was this type of woman.

I don't know if I was thinking about the incident as much as I was feeling it. It was a gut hurt. It wasn't just the embarrassment of acting childish, it was the realization that my behavior projected a much different image than I had of myself. I wasn't like the rest of the guys, or at least that's what I thought.

"What's on tap for the evening's festivities?" inquired Jimmy D.

"Is that even a question?" asked Tommy, taking pride in implying anything having to do with alcohol.

"Another night of debauchery fellas," answered Chris, effectively summing up what everyone was thinking. I didn't feel like drinking, but I had nothing else to do. There was no other outlet for my kind of melancholy.

Among our friends, we had adopted the personas that were laid upon us, as though our friends provided the proper compass of who we really were. The truth is, no one really knew anybody because we didn't really know ourselves, so we made every effort to appease our buddies through devilish pursuits. Any contributions we made to society became nullified through our mission to revolt from it, even though our upbringing didn't justify the behavioral incongruities.

The group had a hierarchy of leadership, but the hierarchy wasn't vertical. It was more like a honeycomb of unique personalities; each person perceiving the other differently, everyone elbowing for a comfortable place in the hive. Outwardly, I was the prototypical college prep: an award recipient of a Presidential Scholarship for academics, an electrical engineering major, a volunteer, a class officer, and a tutor. On the one hand, the boys looked at me like I was Wally Cleaver on Andro. On the other hand, I had a very worldly addiction to materialism and entertainment—I just didn't recognize it. I lusted, in mostly subtle ways, after the two Ws: Wealth and Women. My childhood in a lower income household created a hypnotic attraction to wealth. More than a life of luxury, wealth represented freedom from the weight of financial restriction. My father worked eighty hours per week in a factory and in a restaurant kitchen to put food on the table, and I convinced myself that I was not going to live that life. The allure blossomed from a sense of anticipation because I felt I was on a collision course for success. I had never really failed at anything in my short life.

Chasing women was an altogether different matter. From very early on I desired a wife and a family, an ideal not universally adopted by my hombres, but I wasn't quite sure what that meant for my behavior. When you're eighteen, do you just wait it out, or is there some kind of preparation? To be more exact, I wondered what role a woman plays in the life of a young man. When you are too young to marry, and too old to be mothered, how do you relate to women? Unlike my buddy Chris, I wasn't consumed by the pursuit of carnal lust; I was drawn to the gamesmanship of charming women. As a formal rite of passage, some ancient American Indian tribes required a young man to kill a large animal single-handedly before allowing him to marry. My rite of passage, my artificial threshold for manhood, began and ended with the affections of women. They became the hunted in a game of self-actualization. In other words, I wanted to be *wanted*; I felt empowered by it.

College is a gentlemen's purgatory, and every boy confronts the anxieties of manhood with varying degrees of preparation. Some internalize their issues, wallowing in depression and self-loathing, while others lash out in self-destructive behavior. It is said that men are hard-wired for conflict, but when there is no healthy outlet for masculine energy, the aggression is unleashed in less than admirable ways. We wanted to be seen as warriors and free spirits, like William Wallace or James Dean, but we grew up on Toys 'R Us, piano lessons, and birthday parties at Chuck E. Cheese. We didn't know how to properly mature, and a piece of us yearned for a more troubled past to justify our pugnacity. There's a reason why the movie *Fight Club* resonates so strongly with college males.

There is the other group too, of course. Young men with a castrated masculinity who, like domesticated house cats, have been socially bred as passive softies; men without a backbone, whose feel-good lifestyle lacks strength of character and purpose. Both extremes can be characterized by a considerable deficiency in virtue. In the middle lay the ideal—men with conviction, men with values, men with a humility that surrenders itself to a higher power—men from 1950s movies. Discovering this inner nobility required a courage that lay hidden beneath layers of false, modernist logic.

My malaise never reached a boiling point like some of the others, never overstepped the boundaries of devil-may-care to misdemeanor. Instead, it festered somewhere between the extremes of knight and barbarian—not all bad, but not nearly good enough. Whatever the personal affliction, the boys in my crew were joined through the common bond of college partying. We enjoyed the escapism of it, confronting our struggles by "getting away from it all."

After returning to the dorm, I led the charge toward drunkenness, cracking the first beer against a hip-hop beat and aggressively instigating the revelry. I wanted the night to begin in a desperate way so I could fade into the background, away from my interior conflict. The cheap imitation brew tasted bitter, but I swallowed it like pain medicine for my discomfort. Mickey set the table for Flip Cups (a two-team drinking race) and it became our game of choice for the night. It provided an outlet for our competitive nature, though we didn't realize that the combination of beat-driven music, alcohol, and trash talk only pumped up our aggression. Drunk and loud, we volleyed friendly rounds of cuss words and lewd one-liners.

At first, it was adolescent showboating and humor that instigated the crudeness of our babble, but it eventually began to shape us, particularly as it related to sex. Our perversions blossomed into obsession. Like Pavlov's dog, we would salivate at the thought of satiating our lust, especially because the impressionable college girls made themselves readily available. Our thoughts shaped our words, and our words required action as a stamp of authenticity. To my astonishment, women would willingly canter into our web of fantasy, as though it were the only way to receive attention or be valued. Britney Spears is a great example of this. When she first arrived on the music scene she was a cute sixteen-year-old girl flirting with sexual innuendos in a Catholic schoolgirl outfit while promoting her virginity. Not long after she was seductively panting "I'm a slave for you" while wearing a thong on the outside of her pants. We loved her for this, and Britney loved that we loved her for it. But though we lusted after her, none of us would consider her the type of woman we would bring home to mama, which was the telltale sign of respect and admiration.

Our conversations during drinking games were always brief, and often circular, which is to say they were riddled with contradictions. If we loved something, it was quite possible that we hated it to an equal degree. We loved hooking up, but we had no respect for "sluts." We enjoyed being drunk, but we would laugh at and ridicule people for being drunk. It was as though we were always giving in to social pressure, seeking popularity without becoming a laughing stock.

Alcohol was the great facilitator of our behavior—the hooking up, the aggression, all of it. It gave us courage to overcome our insecurities, and the freedom to act without the weight of accountability. It was easy to justify misbehavior by saying something else made you do it, like having a lucid dream when you can do anything you want because you know you are dreaming.

Another catalyst for our misbehavior was the need for acceptance. Some of us were still virgins, and many of us had never tried drugs or done a lot of drinking. But in college, bad behavior is glamorized by everyone and everything around you. It was good to be bad. What at one time stretched well beyond the boundaries of what we thought was right we began to legitimize through the all-too cliché argument of normalcy. *Everybody's doing it.* Everyone was drinking and having sex. Every magazine, every TV show, every movie, every billboard, every commercial, everything around us promoted sex and booze. The experts encouraged "healthy" sexual activity, as long as it was "safe," as though protection against physical harm could also ward off emotional or spiritual problems. When the Internet launched porn into every dorm room in the 1990s, it brought much more than naked photos of women. Lesbians. Bestiality. Sodomy. Sadomasochism. Though we all agreed that these practices were filthy, in a very scary way we became desensitized to it, and joked about it unendingly. Still worse, we measured our actions against the lowest dregs of society, so our concept of virtue meant staying away from these disordered extremes instead of gravitating to examples of true manhood.

None of this registered with me on Saturday nights. It may have flitted across my mind on Sunday afternoons, or even during a weekday, but never on Saturday nights. By the twelfth game of Flip Cups with Mickey and the gang, I really wasn't giving much thought to anything. I felt a sense of relief and comfort in getting back to an illusory state of freedom. I was addicted to it—not to alcohol, but to the feeling of being totally without responsibility.

"Tommy, I'm feeling itchy, let me touch your man-boob," ribbed Chris, making fun of Tommy and cracking a homosexual joke all in one sentence.

"Mickey, throw me one," barked Johnny, whose beer was empty.

"F— you, Chris. You'd like that, wouldn't you? Go home and throw on Beaches and get back to being gay."

"SO WHAT YOU WANNA DO? . . .TURN OFF THE LIGHTS AND CLOSE THE DOORS/BUT (BUT WHAT?) WE DON'T LOVE THEM HOES, YEAH!" rapped Snoop Dogg, as "Gin and Juice" blared through the sound system. It was three years old, but it was still a party favorite.

"What?"

"Throw me one, you deaf f—!"

"We're out, douche bag. Don't get your panties in a bunch."

"Dude, you're f—ing with me. We bought five cases!" Johnny couldn't believe it: One hundred and twenty beers, ten guys, three and a half hours.

"We are getting f—d-up tonight boys!!" shouted Bobby at the accomplishment.

"What's next? I'm thirsty!" asked Johnny.

"Let's just head down to Cherry Street," lobbied Bobby, referring to a house of seniors on Cherry Street who threw parties nearly every weekend to pay for rent. We weren't old enough to get into any bars, and only a few of us had fake IDs.

"F— that! That place is always a dude fest," argued Chris, referring to the fact that there was never a favorable ratio of guys to girls. "I wanna get laid tonight."

"The only action you're getting tonight is from your room-mate," jabbed Tommy. Jimmy D chimed in with the first decent alternative, mentioning a small party he'd been invited to by a female classmate. Apparently there would be some girls there, and that was all we needed to hear.

"I'm game. They better have beer," approved Bobby, insinuating that the alcohol was more important than the women, which we all knew couldn't be further from the truth.

The walk to the party in no way had a sobering effect on us. It served to give our bodies time to fully absorb all the beer we had just consumed, and it was evident because the group was getting increasingly rowdy. Three of the guys tackled Tommy on the Quad, and he now had grass in his hair and mud stains on his pants. Mickey brought a roadie of Fruit Punch Gatorade and Absolut, and it was being passed around like a joint at a Phish concert. Of course, it was being spilled everywhere, too, so several of the guys had red stains on their shirts. It was a twenty-minute walk in the bitter New England cold to apartment 24C on Lake Street, and the anxiety was heavy. We wanted beer, noise, and women, but as we approached the door, there was little sign of anything. We didn't see any cars. There were only a few lights on in the entire complex, and barely any signs of life. The place was dead.

"Are you f—ing kidding me, Jimmy??"

"What the f—??"

Jimmy D was feeling the heat, knowing that he was on the hook for the twenty-minute walk and the quality of this "party." To make matters worse, he didn't even really know the girl aside from a two-minute conversation after class on Friday. He was in an uncomfortable spot. It took about five seconds before we conceded defeat, so the rest of us hung back as Jimmy walked up to the door, fulfilling his obligatory duty. To our astonishment, Jimmy's girl actually answered, but you could tell by the look on her face that she didn't expect ten of us. Jimmy shot a quick glance over to the group—clearly, something was up. The slow, single-file entrance out of the cold into the small apartment was nothing short of awkward. The apartment was tiny, and six women sat around a coffee table drinking wine coolers, accompanied by two less-than-cool guys drinking Labatt's Blue. The soft background music was barely discernable, but I could make out "Friday I'm in Love" by The Cure.

"Come on in guys. The more the merrier. You're in luck, we just bought a case of beer!" She made every effort to seem nice, but it was clear that she was ill prepared for the numbers. Normally, her comment would have sparked a laugh, but our attention was fixed squarely on the one thing that would save Jimmy's rep; three of the consensus top five women on The Dream Team were present in the living room trying to digest the invasion. The first one I saw was Judy the Beauty, and then the Cookie Monster. I didn't recognize any of the other women until I turned around to see none other than Orange Cardigan Girl.

"Hey, I remember you! Are you feeling alright?" asked OCG sympathetically, referring to the one thing I was hoping to permanently forget. I couldn't believe I had run into her for the second night in a row. She never went out. I tried to act as sober as possible, knowing that fate had presented me an opportunity to remedy my depression from the night before. Here I had the chance to make a proper re-introduction. Though forming my words became an increasingly heavier task, the second night of back-to-back heavy drinking always seemed more forgiving. It was like my body would summon Bill Belichick to make some half-time defensive adjustments. If I tried hard enough, I felt like I could act normally.

"Yeah, much better, thanks. Sorry about—" Tommy somersaulted over a kitchen chair and interrupted my first sentence.

"Nothing to see here! As you were," shouted Tommy, trying to make light of the situation. I'm not sure the girls really knew what to think. It's possible they enjoyed the infusion of a little excitement into an otherwise dull party, but I think they worried about the preservation of their quaint apartment from a bunch of rambunctious strangers, led by Tommy Boy himself, who never met a piece of furniture he couldn't fall through. The guys clearly hated us.

Tommy's fall sparked a chain of embarrassing events. Bobby would end up puking in the bathroom before falling asleep in the bathtub. Chris made no provision for the company and continuously shouted inappropriate comments to the other guys, and Mickey fired up another sloppy drinking game that no one seemed to get into, before quickly complaining that all the free beer was gone. None of it really mattered, though. I was totally consumed in my conversation with OCG.

"I apologize for my Neanderthal friends. They just discovered fire a couple of hours ago and they're pretty excited," I continued, selling them up the river. It was moments like this that I desperately tried to separate myself from my "close" buddies, not because they were bad guys necessarily, but because I didn't want their behavior to reflect negatively on me. The power a beautiful woman holds over a man is a mystifying thing. In a moment it can turn a meathead into a rose-toting emotional clone of Michael Bolton.

"No need to apologize. They're funny," OCG politely responded, which was a nice way of saying she was embarrassed for me. She didn't seem wildly interested in the conversation, but I continued to probe.

"I'm Tarek, by the way. You?" I asked as if I didn't already know her real name was Lauryn.

"What is it?" she asked.

"Ta-a-a-r-e-h-k" I replied, elongating each syllable.

"How do you spell it?"

"T. A. R. E. K. It's kind of weird."

"It's unique. I'm Lauryn. Where are you from?"

"New Bedford, Massachusetts." I was keeping the answers short, testing my ability to sound coherent.

"No, I mean, where is your family from?" she asked, somewhat engaged at this point. I had my foot in the door. We were already discussing *la familia*, which meant I could ask about hers without coming across too creepy. I wanted to know everything about her.

"My father is from Lebanon and my mother is Portuguese. And you?"

"Half-Irish, half-Scottish. Hence the pasty white skin."

I loved her self-deprecating humor. She was gorgeous, but not a Maxim Cover Girl or a Playmate. Her looks were classically sophisticated, like Princess Isabelle in Braveheart, but plain enough to be easily approachable. Lauryn confidently locked onto me with electric, bright green eyes, and at each slight turn of the head, her hair would emit a fruity fragrance that would reset my senses like sorbet at fancy restaurant. Sadly, I was so caught up in my appreciation of her that I failed to formulate an interesting response. Dead spots were terrible. Nothing kills a good conversation like dead spots. Like a game of chess you

need to think three steps ahead, continuously lining up interesting things to say—questions, anecdotes, whatever. I had nothing
at this point, and the alcohol wasn't doing me any favors.

"I love Ireland." I knew it was lame the second I said it.

"Really? Have you been there?" she asked, sounding moder-
ately excited.

"No, but I want to. It looks incredible in pictures," I replied,
offering another gem of a response.

"Oh, you'd love it."

"Yeah." More silence. This time the game was over; I could
feel it. Fisk had rounded third. I felt like Larry Legend in the '91
Pacers series—she wasn't seeing me in my prime. Rather than
brainstorming something to say, in painful self-awareness I dwelt
upon the rapid disintegration of the dialogue. I couldn't shake
it; the silence was killing me.

"Well, I don't know what else to say." I had to say something
to break the silence, but I put the nail in my own coffin. Could I
have possibly made the situation worse? Why did alcohol always
open the floodgates to the uncouth?

"Do you have any brothers or sisters?" she sprightly asked,
pulling out the defibrillators to resurrect the conversation. Most
girls would have pushed the eject button at that point, fleeing the
scene as quickly as possible, but Lauryn was different than most
girls. She possessed a motherly quality. I don't know if she took
pity on me or if she was genuinely interested, but I was back in
the game.

"Yeah, I have an older sister. We're really close," I offered,
making the first slight allusion to a non-superficial topic. It was
dangerous territory given my condition. "You?"

"I'm the eldest of nine. I would say I'm probably the closest
to my brother Joseph, who was second."

"Wow, how did you like coming from a big family?"

"I wouldn't trade it for the world. It's awesome. Ya know, never a dull moment. Do you see yourself having a lot of kids?" The question threw me for a loop. That wasn't a normal question, at least not one that I was used to, especially from a girl I'd just met at a college party. I couldn't help wondering if she was sizing me up. A girl like Lauryn has a list, I figured, of what she wants in a guy, and perhaps this was a salvo intended to see if I was worth her time. The mere reference to having kids had me excited.

"Hi, I'm Jess!" At that moment, the hostess interrupted, and my body language likely indicated that I wanted her to leave me to my soul mate. "Can I get you anything?"

"Yeah, I'd love a water. Thanks." I had to make the switch to stay afloat, plus beer breath was an omnipresent concern. Returning my attention to Lauryn, I proudly announced the one answer I knew would assuredly have her ovaries in a tizzy. "I want a ton of kids. Fourteen, fifteen, whatever. I want a full quiver."

"Really? You don't hear too many guys saying that." I was *so* in.

"Well, I'm different than most guys." I'm sure it sounded cheesy, but enough like a soap opera to keep her intrigued.

"Did I hear you say you wanted fourteen kids?" an astonished Jess questioned loudly when returning with my bottle of Poland Spring. I was angry that she made such a big scene about it because I didn't want her to blow my cover with the fellas, and I most certainly didn't want her to invite herself back into the conversation.

"Yeah, why not?"

"Why not?" Jess repeated. "Have you ever had a kid? Try having one before you commit to fourteen. Besides, haven't you ever heard of overpopulation?"

I took the last comment as a direct affront to Lauryn and her family of nine. It was my first opportunity to rise to her defense.

"Overpopulation is a myth. Every single person in the world could live comfortably in the state of Texas."

"Yeah, but who'd want to?" Jess responded as she walked away, either not looking for a fight or not having an argument.

"Are you serious about having all those kids?" asked Lauryn, sounding more inquisitive with each question.

"Absolutely. Don't you?" I knew she'd say yes.

"Heck no. Two tops. One boy and one girl."

"What?! I thought you just said you loved having a big family."

"I did. I love my family, but that doesn't mean I want as many kids as my mother. I've seen what it did to her body. I'm not going through that."

I couldn't believe what I was hearing.

"But isn't that kind of selfish?" I wondered aloud.

"Maybe to you, but you're not the one having them."

"Yeah, but you think weighing a few pounds less would bring you as much joy as a child?"

"It's not just the weight, it's the time. I still want to be able to work, and I still want to look good for my husband. Why are we even having this conversation?" She suddenly seemed agitated. I wanted to drop the topic as well. It seemed so bizarre to me that the eldest girl from a large family would care more about her figure and her career than having children. I could understand an only child holding that position, or someone from a small family, but I would have expected a different perspective on ideal family life coming from her.

"Interesting." I started to feel dizzy between the beer, the lively discussion, and the proximity to my dream girl, so I made more of an effort to be still.

We spent the next half-hour steering clear of controversy, focusing on things like taste in music, favorite movies, food preferences, pet peeves, and other superficial topics, until finally she returned to the one subject she couldn't seem to shake.

"So, how are you going to feel when your wife is huge after all those kids?"

"You really don't believe me do you?"

"Absolutely not."

"I'd love her either way. There's always going to be someone younger and prettier out there, whether she has one kid or ten."

"Yeah, you say that now."

"And I'll say that at the altar."

"We'll see."

"We will see." As a result of the stalemate we were officially flirting.

"And what if your wife wants to use birth control?" she continued, trying to gauge the consistency of my responses.

"She wouldn't."

"How do you know?"

"Because I wouldn't marry her if she did."

"Yeah, right! You mean to tell me that if you found the right girl you wouldn't marry her just because she wanted to use birth control?"

"She wouldn't be the right girl, obviously." The irony of my response was that I wasn't entirely sold on the strength of my convictions, though I clung to my argument. Fortunately, we focused solely on the "what," never continuing down the path of the "why."

"Isn't that a little hypocritical of you to say? You're using some kind of birth control now, obviously."

"What makes you say that?"

"It's a small school, Tar-eek," she replied, mispronouncing my name.

"What are you trying to say?"

"I know you've hooked up with girls," she stated, confirming my fears while rendering impotent the sliver of confidence I had. In our college-speak, a "hook-up" meant, at the very least, kissing.

"Yeah, but I'm not proud of it. If I could do it over again I would've done things differently in a heartbeat. I get lonely sometimes, and it's hard," I countered, pleading guilty to the charges of immoral behavior, but attempting to justify my actions.

"Lonely? Gimme a break."

"Well it's not like I have my family around dropping some love. People need a good power hug once in awhile."

"Apparently more than a power hug."

"Yeah, but I've never had sex. I'm still holding out for marriage." It was the first time I'd admitted that to anyone, and I realized the hypocrisy of the statement the second I said it. I wanted to shine a light on something I considered to be virtuous, but I only dug myself a deeper grave.

"You're such a liar!" she replied in laughter and disbelief. "Like I believe that. You talk such a good game about how you want to have kids and be a dad, and how you're a virgin and this and that. Meanwhile, you and your guy friends go out and get drunk and puke on lawns and hook up with all sorts of girls. I'm sure your wife would appreciate that, Prince Charming." Her tone was still very playful, but plainly matter-of-fact. The truth stung. Just when I thought I had her stepping away for a second from her feminist views on marriage, I failed to recognize my own dissonant conduct. By presenting the irrefutable argument that actions speak louder than words, she rightfully disputed my authenticity. As a man, I had let her down as much as she had let me down.

It became clear to me that Lauryn had written off the possibility that men existed like the one I was attempting to pass off as me. Deep down, it seemed as though she wanted that guy to exist, but she feared the change his existence would bring about for her, and thus rejected all allusions to the actuality of this imaginary superman.

"What do you think happiness is, Lauryn?"

"What?"

I repeated the question, a lost sheep trying to salvage hope.

"Living each day like it's your last, never having any regrets, and always having someone to love," she pontificated. But the puppy-calendar clichés just didn't resonate with me. They couldn't cut through my shell of uncertainty and dissatisfaction. The doorbell rang, and a smug-looking senior entered the apartment in a hockey pullover. He looked familiar, but I had never met him before. As he approached us, he carried an empty beer in his left hand while prepping a can of Skoal in his right, and through a friend I later discovered that he'd hooked up with several of the women in the freshmen dorm.

"Hi Billy!" Lauryn excitedly shouted. "Tar-eek. This is my boyfriend."

breakdown

G OOD MORNING, good morning everyone!" greeted Professor McDowell, even though it was actually noon, and
therefore technically too late for him to be saying *good
morning*. Mondays were my worst day of the week because I had
four classes and a three-hour Physics lab. By the fourth class I
was inevitably starving and very focused on lunch. Twice per
week the entire freshmen class attended Humanities Lecture in
a large auditorium, and the professors in the department rotated
the duties of lecturing on the readings. There were a few mum-
mies in the department, but Professor McDowell was a younger
guy in his mid-thirties, and he understood the necessity of being
energetic when delivering a lecture to a group of eighteen- and
nineteen-year-olds.

"Today, of course, we are dealing with *Aristotle*," he opened,
emphasizing the word Aristotle as though he could sense he
was delivering bad news. "We will be spending a considerable
amount of time reviewing his famous work, *Nichomachean Eth-*

ics, a work that many consider to be his greatest work. Glancing ahead, later on this year we will read St. Thomas Aquinas, and it has often been said that St. Thomas *Christianized* Aristotle's work by connecting Aristotelian philosophy to Christian theology."

They say a good speaker can make anything sound interesting, but there's something about philosophy on a Monday afternoon that's about as exciting as the televised World Billiard Championships on ESPN2. The weekend had exhausted everyone. I peered down the long row of my friends in the upper deck, and the body language said it all—heads buried beneath hats and hoodies, eyes closed, bodies slouched deeply into bright blue chairs. The attendance was sparse, a consequence of flu season and the cold, grey February afternoon. There were two types of student in the audience: the guiltless underachievers who attended simply to say they went, and the incessant note-takers who never seemed to understand anything but always tested well.

A heavy fatigue settled in right behind my retinas, the type that won't let you sleep but leaves you continuously wiped-out. Like a Prozac-popping insomniac, I felt alert and alone. I obsessed over Saturday's conversation with my faux dream girl, and the discovery that my life was on autopilot. Whatever control I had, I gave up freely to my friends in return for their short-term admiration. I lacked any sense of purpose.

The night before, I had attended Mass during one of the few hours I was awake. It was common for several of my friends and me to attend Mass on our Catholic campus, but it wasn't a sense of deep religiosity that drove us there. Mass on campus was a social event. It was held late Sunday evening, and it provided one last opportunity to "people watch" before the weekend was out. Our attendance was downright hypocritical, like a gang lord or mafioso baptizing his child. I think most of us liked the idea of worship; we just never liked the demands that came with it. Still, I would dutifully attend church because I felt obligated to be there, but I always left unaffected.

As I stared at the podium, a tangible depression settled in. I sat up straight in my chair humbly attempting to fight it off. My mind tried to drum up anything that might offer a solution, but I was unsure where to look. I was eighteen and broke. I had nothing to offer a woman. My grades were barely average, and the NBA wasn't exactly pounding on my door. I was in no man's land, so I placed all of my faith in the future, daydreaming about how different life would be once I had a job.

"Today, I really want to focus on the topic of *happiness*. What is happiness, according to Aristotle?" asked McDowell.

I snapped to attention. The topic was a little ironic. I felt caught in the middle of a weird *Twilight Zone* episode, thinking I might turn around to discover that everyone in the audience was suddenly headless. It seemed as though the professor had specifically prepared the lecture for me after hearing about my conversation from the weekend. It was like randomly quoting a 1980s movie and seeing it suddenly appear on TNT.

"What is happiness?" McDowell repeated. His delivery was animated, and there was so much inflection in his tone that his speech seemed more like a dramatic performance than a lecture. "Is there a difference between happiness and pleasure? Aristotle would emphatically say 'YES!' Happiness—or *Eudaemonia* in Greek—describes that general feeling of peace and contentment in life, that positive sense of self-worth . . . the *joie de vivre*, as they say in French . . . the highest good that we all aim to achieve. He defines happiness as, I quote: 'the exercise of the soul's faculties in conformity with virtue in a complete life.' Unquote. Don't worry; I'll explain that in a minute. First, what makes this different than pleasure? Ah! Well pleasure, you see, does not have the lasting effects of happiness, because all pleasure is temporal. It is gone in an instant. (Snapping his fingers). Furthermore, pleasure is not a unique thing; it's a by-product of something else. You might receive pleasure from eating or making love, but you cannot receive that pleasure without the activity it is tied to. The two cannot be separated. Happiness, on the other hand, is a continuous activity of the soul. It is not a by-product of some other activity."

I didn't take any notes. Instead, I drew pictures on my notepad as a way for my brain to digest the philosophical meaning. A shroud of silence covered the audience, a stark deviation from the noisy days of September. In the midst of the stillness, I sat fixated on the professor's words. The philosophy felt pertinent, it felt accessible. Rather than a strictly academic exercise, it was as though I was listening to the Boy Scouts' manual for the completely incompetent.

"Now, let's stop for a second. What's he trying to say?" questioned McDowell, and like any quality professor, he drew us aside to explain the message in layman's terms. "I have a pen here. What's the purpose of this pen?? [Pause] To WRITE! The unique function of this object is for writing. Therefore, I know I have a good pen if it writes well. We are able to discern the excellence —or arête in Greek—of the pen by whether or not it performs its function properly."

All of a sudden I had no idea where he was going with this.

"Well, then, what is the unique function of *man*?" he asked rhetorically. Then, softening to a whisper, answered his own question: "*To reason* . . . You see, Aristotle would say the success of man's ability to live the excellent, virtuous life determines his happiness. As I stated earlier, happiness is the exercise of the soul's faculties—the intellectual faculty, which is the ability to reason, and the moral faculty, which is the ability to make rational judgment. If the soul functions in accordance with virtue over the span of a life, it is then that happiness is achieved and it is then that humanity comes in closest contact with the divine."

According to Aristotle, my definition of happiness was off, as was my strategy. Of all the pieces that I felt were necessary in the puzzle of life, virtue was not at the top of the list. Though I'd always assumed I would try to live a life of virtue, try to be a "good person," I did not see it as a pre-requisite for obtaining my ultimate desires.

My other mistake seemed to be in the approach. Rather than working towards a "state of being," I made every effort to connect moments of pleasure in continuous succession in order to fabricate a sense of fake happiness. When the moments of pleasure fled, they took with them any lease I had on happiness. Like a junkie, I became addicted to my fix, because without pleasure I was totally miserable. These pleasures weren't x-rated—I wasn't shooting heroin or sleeping in brothels—but they weren't edifying either. They consisted of television and music and video games and drinking and the Internet. They had become needs. My life was a constant stream of distraction.

My thoughts darted forward, drawing one conclusion after another. I decided that through my addiction I became egotistical; I was selfish. If it wasn't good for me, I didn't care about what it did to other people. This was especially true in my relationships with women. In a certain sense, I was guilty of robbery. I used women. By objectifying them, it became much easier to receive pleasure from them without the guilt of emotional or mental pain.

Yes, I understood the philosophy. Happiness requires effort, a life-long process of training and discipline. It forces a person to live life according to an ideal, toward the pursuit of perfection. Though pleasure is a by-product of virtue, virtue doesn't demand it, in the same way that food doesn't require a pleasant taste to be nourishing. Pleasure is everywhere; it's readily available for everyone, but most especially in the United States and other overdeveloped countries. My generation, I figured, and to a large extent my parent's generation, had lived out the dream, from a materialistic standpoint, that was only vaguely imagined by the previous one hundred generations. But pleasure is not an end, so I concluded that a life spent pursuing pleasure, like a donkey chasing a carrot, would always lack direction.

I just couldn't fully grasp the word "divine," especially the Christian definition. What did McDowell mean by that? How is faith to be understood in the modern world? It's the Internet and Range Rovers versus Incarnation and Resurrection; Big Macs and Slurpees versus transubstantiation; Michael Jordan versus Michael the Archangel; Billy Madison versus the Bible; Virgin Records versus the Virgin Mary. Embracing Christian doctrine as an adult was so mystical and unfathomable that I subconsciously reduced my faith to the lesser subcategory of values. Values I could readily understand. *Be good to people. Love your neighbor. Do unto others, as you would have them do unto you.* But the connection between values, happiness, and salvation remained for me largely ambiguous.

"In conclusion, I want to leave you with my favorite passages from the text, which I'm sure you are all now dying to read!" McDowell continued. My mind had wandered through a large part of the professor's lecture, and it neared its conclusion. "Aristotle writes: 'The happy man, then, as we define him will preserve his character; for he will be occupied continually in excellent deeds and excellent speculations; and, whatever his fortune be, he will take it in the noblest fashion, and bear himself always and in all things suitably, since he is truly good.' He goes on to say, 'And if it is what a man does that determines the character of his life, then no happy man will become miserable; for he will never do what is hateful and base. For we hold that the man who is truly wise and good will bear with dignity whatever fortune sends, and always make the best of his circumstances, as a good general will turn the forces at his command to the best account, and a good shoemaker will make the best shoe that can be made . . . if this be so, the happy man will never become miserable.' Thank you for your attentiveness. Have an excellent afternoon!"

Thirty minutes after class I sat in silence on the couch, staring at a soggy tuna sandwich in the dark emptiness of my cluttered dorm room. I felt numb. It was as though the sensory overload of my life had left me calloused, like the fingers of a guitar player who had plucked a chord one too many times. In the quiet of that place, my throat tightened and my nostrils flared, and with every last ounce of my manhood I fought off the emotional swell.

I had entered an honest and vulnerable place, a place that is difficult to find in the forest of overabundance. It's a place you seek mostly in the alone times, like when you are lost in the middle of nowhere or on the brink of death or struggling with depression. It's then that you discover that, imprinted on your heart, is a natural calling towards something higher. I was confronted with the only question that seemed to matter: Is there a God?

As an altar boy for ten years, as a Catholic, as someone with a tendency for introspection, I had never really denied a belief in God. My problem was that I didn't know *why*. How could I be sure that He actually existed? Twice in my life I had been duped into believing in a false deity who possessed great superpowers.

My first lesson occurred at the age of eight when my sister broke the news that the myth of Santa Claus was one big conspiracy. (In fact, she made me privy to the royal triumvirate of lies that included the fallacy of the Easter Bunny and the Tooth Fairy). My parents, teachers, the media—everyone was an accomplice. I would spend my entire year wishing and hoping for Santa, and I kept lists of all the good deeds I'd performed, from doing my chores to taking my bath to being good to my sister. I wrote it all down and sent him letters. To discover that it was all one clever ploy in a Clancy-esque cover-up was earth shattering to me.

The second time was less climactic. It happened slowly over a period of several adolescent years when it registered that my parents were not perfect. As a young child, I viewed my parents as the living manifestations of God Himself, because my existence depended entirely on their power. They had created me. As I began to realize their imperfections, my trust in them waned accordingly, and any confidence I placed in something outside of me became shaken.

So as I stared at my tuna sandwich, I was forced to ask myself: What prevented someone, the Church let's say, from one day unlocking the secret of a gigantic piece of fiction? The motives were there—money, control, power, etc. The fear of being deceived was almost as frightening as the fear of Godlessness. Was I placing my hope in a fantasy? How could anyone be assured of God's existence?

I opted to break into the jumbo-sized Costco box of Goldfish in my trunk. I shoved so many goldfish into my mouth at one time that it formed a Playdough-like cracker concoction, and in the process of trying to defeat this sticky mass, I dwelt on the bleak alternative: *Without God, I am nothing more than processed meat, a glorified hot dog soon to be consumed.*

three

science fiction

I HATED PHYSICS LAB. Though it was refreshing to tackle a subject that offered clear right and wrong answers, the topics seemed totally useless. *Calculate the ballistic trajectory from point A to point B of a cannonball shot at such and such an angle . . . what is the acceleration of Object X ten feet from the surface of the earth if it possesses such and such surface area . . . what is the mass of the lead weight on pulley C if the weight on pulley A is such and such . . blah . . blah . . blah.* Did anyone actually calculate this stuff by hand anymore? There was no chance I would ever use any of it.

As if the subject matter wasn't rough enough, the students in class offered little redeeming value on the social front. I never noticed any of them around campus, yet for some reason they would magically appear in class on a mission with their TI-82 calculator. Only eighteen of us remained from the thirty-one who started the year.

Our instructor, Professor Davis, loved Physics. He was difficult, he was by the book, but when it came to force, mass, and acceleration, he was like Dick Vitale on crack—all fired up. Undoubtedly, he had a little Nutty Professor in him, but his quirks made him interesting.

Professor Davis stepped into the room with a Bunsen burner, a frying pan, and an egg, and he began cooking the egg silently in order to build the anticipation.

"Does anyone know what I'm demonstrating?" he opened.

"Acting like an idiot," whispered my lab partner, Charlie, sitting directly behind me.

"Yes, Kim!"

"How to cook an egg?" she answered. Kim never missed a class, and she made every effort to be the teacher's pet.

"Ah, the obvious answer. Yeeessss, but what else? Anybody? . . . ENERGY!!" he shouted excitedly, as though the word *energy* was suddenly a verb that could be used to describe an activity. "It's the number one topic in America today."

I glanced over at my lab partner with a puzzled look. I wasn't sure if, in his alt scientific universe, he'd surmised that the general populace was suddenly passionate about physics.

"Think about it," he continued, "From gasoline, to electricity, to dieting—everything is about energy!"

"Dieting?" Kim asked out loud.

"Sure. How many times have you looked on the side of a can of food to see how many calories it contains? Calories are a measure of energy. If you eat too many calories, your body stores the energy in the form of fat. If you eat too few calories, your body will burn off fat to get the energy it needs to function. That's why people who are trying to lose weight exercise. They want to burn off their energy reserves."

"What does this have to do with the egg?" inquired Kim, trying to provide the professor an easy transition into his class experiment.

"Well, let's take a look here. There is kerosene attached to the burner, representing a store of potential energy. When I ignite the burner, that energy is then transferred in the form of heat, or kinetic energy. The energy is not eliminated; it simply changes form. We call this the Conservation of Energy, the principle that the total energy of a system, potential energy plus kinetic energy, remains constant. And what about the egg? Well, this cooked egg represents a certain amount of energy, about ninety calories to be exact, or 360 kilojoules. When we eat this egg, it will function in the same way that the kerosene did for the Bunsen burner. Do you follow? This should be a review for everyone here because you have all seen this in high school."

There was a giant clock next to the door in the Physics lab. Four minutes had passed. Two hours and fifty-six minutes to go.

"Don't think I'm letting you off easy; this is just the beginning because we are going to take this concept one step further. You will investigate the law of energy conservation by measuring the transfer of gravitational potential energy to kinetic energy."

Just as my mind began to trail off into its vacuous nether regions, something clicked with me - Conservation of Energy. I seized the opportunity to challenge the good professor.

"Professor Davis." I raised my hand as I called out his name. "You're saying that energy is neither created nor destroyed in a closed system."

"Exactly."

"Well, is the same thing true in the entire universe? I mean, is the amount of energy in the universe a constant?"

"That's what scientists believe."

"Well, if energy can't be created, how did it originate in the first place?"

Professor Davis paused to think about the question, and then chuckled. "That's a debate for another day, or maybe another class even. Let's just try to stay on the topic at hand. We have a lot to cover."

His non-answer was an answer in itself, and my mind continued to linger on theology. I never understood the logic in the "Creation without a Creator" argument, not in high school and not now. It seemed to me that in order for the universe to exist in the first place, there must first exist something outside of the universe, as difficult as that was to comprehend. My fragile belief in God remained active on this point alone. I could only rationalize three possibilities:

1. Either someone or something created the universe, which acknowledges science's boundaries and threatens atheism.

2. The universe created itself, which immediately fails under the scientific principle that matter and energy cannot be created or destroyed.

3. The universe always existed, a hypothesis that gives inanimate matter the God-like characteristic of infinite existence, attaching a divine quality to matter that is scientifically untenable.

In fact, I concluded that it isn't creationism and science that are at odds, as is often taught; it's that creationism and atheism are at odds. I mulled over this question for the remainder of class.

On my way out of Physics lab, I ran into Randy, a guy I'd met at a Campus Ministry retreat earlier in the year. Unlike Mass, a very small number of students ever attended the college retreats, and I never had any intention of going on one myself. I was lured into it at the urging of Marlene Bayer, a gorgeous senior who caught me off-guard during a chance encounter. She was recruiting bodies to fill spots for the weekend trip, and any bystander in the hallway around the Campus Ministry office became a target. The episode occurred during the first month of school when, as a freshman, I said "yes" to just about anything because I wanted to meet people.

Wanna go to a party? *Definitely.*

Wanna play flag football? *Absolutely.*

Wanna go on a retreat? *Um, well, why the hell not.*

In hindsight, the trip offered a much-needed respite from the first month of college partying, and the long drive through New Hampshire to the coast of Maine was quietly enjoyable. The retreat introduced me to the group of people who tend to fly under the radar until graduation—the wallflowers and the straight-A students, the classmates you never see on the weekends or hanging out at the cafeteria. I didn't want to be a part of their crowd, at least not at that time. I had spent the weekend intentionally reserved, standoffish, almost taunting God to prove to me that the kumbaya-geek-fest offered anything of profound substance. The politeness, the guitar playing, the genuine likeability of the people on the trip, was all very nauseating for a guy who, for the first month of college, had immersed himself in the party life of keg stands and vulgarity. Subconsciously, I did my best to play the Judd Nelson character from *The Breakfast Club*, the guy who shouldn't fit in, who swears for effect, who disdains the thought of being tamed by a group of Puritans. The tune *"One of these things is not like the other, one of these just doesn't belong"* became a self-prescribed soundtrack in my head. I wasn't interested in spiritual reflection, especially not the candy-coated kind. I hadn't come down from the partying high, and I didn't want to.

To make matters worse, Marlene didn't even make the trip.

Randy was a heavy-set, soft-spoken biology major who was neither popular, nor unpopular. No one really knew very much about him, actually. He was a library rat, and though he was naturally gifted, he studied more than anyone else I knew. Randy was the guy who always seemed to have an answer for everything. He was a fifty-year-old in a nineteen-year-old body. He didn't sing, he didn't play games, and he didn't really socialize much on the retreat except for the bonfire gathering on Saturday night. He was a textbook introvert, burying himself in his journal unless someone asked him a direct question. He was personable, but only when a person coaxed him from his introverted world.

I got along with Randy just fine. He had a dry sense of humor like a grandfather would. I would ask him a question like, "Do you have a pen?" and he would answer, "I have a lot of pens." Randy had distanced himself from the retreat as much as I had, but for entirely different reasons. I didn't know him particularly well, but I had the sense that we were kindred spirits in a way, lost in our own divergent thoughts and each withholding the natural version of ourselves.

"What's up, bro?" I asked, running into him after Physics lab.

"The ceiling," he replied casually. "You coming from class?"

"Yeah. Three hours of hell. Hey, are you familiar with Newton's Law, the Conservation of Energy?" The question sounded nerdy, but you can take greater risks when you know the other person has zero influence on your image. Randy was very much into science, so I was confident he knew all about it.

"Sure, I know the basics. Energy can't be created or destroyed," he replied softly.

"Exactly. I've been dwelling on that all afternoon. If that's the case, it seems like it basically makes the case for a Creator. I mean, all the energy in the universe is in flux—moving, changing —but it's not *creating*. It's just transferring what is already there. Do you follow?"

"Sure," he replied, showing no indication that he was surprised by the subject matter, even though we were discussing the origins of the universe just two seconds after a casual hello.

"So basically, where did it all come from, if not from God? Where did all the energy come from?" I knew his answer but I wanted to get his take on things.

"Well, what you're touching on is basically Thomas Aquinas' first couple of proofs for the existence of God called the 'uncaused cause' and the 'unmoved mover.' He has five proofs altogether. We had to memorize all of them in high school. Hey, I'm on my way to the library. You heading that way?"

"Yeah, I'll head over there with you." I had no intention of studying, but I wanted to continue the conversation.

"Basically, he observed that in nature, everything that is moving moves because it has been acted upon by something else. A baseball moves because I throw it, the trees sway because of the wind, etc. Well, if nothing can move itself, there must have been a very first mover—a.k.a. the Unmoved Mover. Same thing is true for creation. Nothing can create itself, because you can't get something out of nothing. Therefore, there must be an original creator that was not created—a.k.a. the Uncaused Cause. This is what we call God."

"If you assume it all came from God, that begs the question, where did God come from?" I said, playing Devil's Advocate.

"He was always there. That's the whole point. You can't have creation if He wasn't."

"Yeah, but how could he always be there? It doesn't make sense. It's impossible."

"It's only impossible if you think God is constrained by the same laws the universe is," he replied, very seriously. "Why can't God exist infinitely? Why should He be constrained by our human understanding, T-Saab?"

"I don't know. My mind just won't go there."

"Look, let's say all of the major events of world history are hash marks on a thermometer, like a timeline in a history book. Well, the passage of time is like the steady, constant rise of the thermometer's mercury. Just like we would read a thermometer, God sees all the hash marks of time in one moment—past, present, and future, even though each moment in history passes only as the mercury rises. Do you follow? When we talk about science, we are talking about what takes place inside the thermometer of time and space. When we talk about God, we are talking about the guy who made the thermometer. People try to analyze God in terms of science, but it's like trying to analyze the carpenter using a rocking chair."

I stared at him blankly but nodded my head in such a way to show him I *kind of* understood.

"What are the other three proofs?"

"I don't really remember them anymore. A couple of them were pretty abstract, and philosophy really isn't my thing. I think the last one was the argument of intelligent design. Aquinas believed that intelligent design was observable in the way non-living objects move towards a certain end—like the moon or the oceans, for example. It doesn't happen randomly."

"It's pretty interesting. I'm just trying to put it all together."

"T, if you need science to prove to you that there is a God, take some time and read up on DNA. Scientists say that the information stored in DNA to create protein structure is more complex than the most incredibly complex computer code. That code isn't random. They're baffled about how that information is written."

"I take it you don't believe in evolution either."

"Well, I believe in some of Darwin's stuff. Survival of the fittest? Definitely. Natural selection? Adaptation? No question about it. But the reason that many scientists doubt the theory of *macro*evolution is mutational theory, which is the idea that a bunch of random mutations over a long period of time can create complex new biological structures. It's scientifically bogus because nearly all mutations are harmful to an organism. Not only that, but the number of mutations it would take to go from protozoa to human is so astronomical it is absolutely impossible. The funny thing is that evolution is so widely embraced by people who have never actually read *The Origin of Species*. There is a world of difference between *micro*evolution and *macro*evolution."

"Interesting."

"But don't get me started. One of the countless other problems is the theory for how life begins. People claim that cells formed naturally out of a 'primordial soup' of life's building blocks. But there is no known chemical process for the natural production of DNA, RNA, or proteins! That's why no one has ever been able to create a living cell in a lab. Even the simplest known bacteria are more complex than the most complex machine. I'm not trying to tell you what to believe, I'd just encourage you to take a look at the scientific facts. They stare us all in the face, but no one cares to think."

"I'll look into it. It was good seeing you, man," I replied. We had arrived at the front door of the library.

"You too. Just remember, scientific theories are like Swiss cheese. Most of them are great, but there are holes everywhere."

good and *not* good

"BOBBY, DO YOU BELIEVE IN GOD?"
My roommate turned around with a puzzled look. It was 12:30 AM and I was ready to crash, but the halls were still echoing with commotion. I had just arrived from another long session in the library preparing for midterms, somersaulting through the doors of reality. The contrast between the silence of the campus library and the rush of my entertainment-driven life presented itself distinctly within the confines of my dorm room. About a week had passed since Professor McDowell's lecture, and I still had God on my mind. At the risk of tanking my exams, I spent more time perusing the shelves of the theology section than I did on math or physics.

"Sure," he offered, non-assertively, in the same way you do when asked if you want ketchup with your fries. Our conversations were always fairly superficial, and my question launched us into uncharted—and uncomfortable—territory.

"Why?"

"Just curious. It's been on my mind lately. I just think it's impossible that there *isn't* a God," I stated, removing the PlayStation controller from my seat.

"Yeah, but I think it's impossible to know for sure though," he countered. "It's just impossible."

"How do you figure? The evidence seems irrefutable. What's the counter-argument?" I asked, baiting him to challenge my position. I wanted to see if my newly formed opinions would hold up.

"The counterargument? The counterargument is that He's not here and we can't know," he explained, attempting to state the obvious.

"Neither is Pam Anderson, but you have no problem worshipping *her*," I quipped.

"It doesn't matter if she exists or not, as long as I have something to look at," he remarked proudly, satisfied with his fantasy.

At that moment, Jimmy D stumbled into the room chewing on a slice of pizza. As he struggled to form his words, a golf ball-sized wad of food impregnated his cheek.

"What's up, fellas?!"

"What's up, Jimmy," we replied in unison.

"What are you guys doin'? You gonna watch SportsCenter?" he asked.

"T is getting all philosophical on me," explained Bobby.

"T-Saab will do that sorta thing. What's the topic?" I brought Jimmy up to speed on the conversation until we were officially entrenched in a debate over God's existence—and, eventually, world religion.

"Look, T, I'm not sayin' there isn't a God. There might very well be. All I'm saying is that it's impossible for us to know anything about Him!" Jimmy stated emphatically. The debate had gone from awkward to aggressive in short order, as debates often did with our clan.

"I have to agree with Jimmy. I think all the world religions are praying to the same God," added Bobby, shaking his head.

"But do you really believe that, Bobby? Some religions believe in ten Gods, some believe in one, some believe there are three in one," I replied, but they held fast to their opinions. Inevitably, the conversation took a very Catholic turn. It was impossible to objectively debate theology apart from our catechetical upbringing because many of our beliefs lay dormant beneath a heavy layer of modernism. Our worldview shaped our Christianity, and not the other way around.

"What does it matter if there are slight differences between this or that? It's all tradition. All the religions basically preach the same dogma. Don't kill. Be good to people. At the very top, they're all praying to the same guy," replied Jimmy.

"But that really makes no sense, Jimmy, if you think about it for more than thirty seconds, bro. Seriously, we have to ask ourselves why God would create human life in the first place," I said.

"Who knows?" said Bobby.

"Somebody's got to. Besides, I think it's pretty obvious—to love and be loved, right? Why else would He create life? It's pretty hard to be loved if people think you are someone different than you are, wouldn't you say?" I asked.

"No."

"Look, we're all Catholic. Either Christ was God Incarnate or He wasn't. That's the bottom line. I'm not trying to be pharisaical, but if you don't believe Christ was God, then I think you're missing the whole point," I said.

"We can ask ourselves these questions all day long, but we're not going to get anywhere, T. I mean, can God make a rock He can't lift? We're just going to go around in circles," replied Jimmy.

"I think there are answers, bro. And no, I don't think God can."

"Okay, well now you're saying God isn't omnipotent."

"No, I'm just saying God can't act contrary to His nature. He's perfect, right? Can a perfect boat sink? Can a perfect rock roll uphill? Of course not. So if God is perfect, He can't limit His perfection. It's like asking me if God can relinquish all His power. He wouldn't be God!"

"Dude, you're killing me," replied Bobby. "Take a breather, brother. Don't we get enough of this s—t in Humanities?"

The discussion reminded me of a reading in our Humanities course entitled *The Marks of an Educated Man* by Alan Simpson, who was the president of Vassar College. In the essay, Simpson noted: "The vital aid to clear thought is the habit of approaching everything we hear and everything we are taught to believe with a certain skepticism. The method of using doubt as an examiner is a familiar one among scholars and scientists, but it is also the best protection that a citizen has against the cant and humbug that surround us."

I remembered that quote distinctly because I had never before viewed the term "skepticism" that way, but his words seemed truer now than ever. For the first time in a long time I began sweeping out the cobwebs of my intellect in order to arrive at some certainty about life. In the same way that a sailor tests the strength of a knot by yanking on it, I had begun spending hours deconstructing my faith as a skeptic, only to build it back up through rational argument. It was an illustration of true learning, because it was more than a simple exercise in processing facts.

"Fellas, forget what people believe for a second. What is truth? That's the real question." I tried to reorient the discussion.

"What is truth? Who are you, Confucius?!" Jimmy responded, leaning back in his chair.

"Do you think God believes murder is wrong?" I asked.

"Sure . . . ," conceded Jimmy.

"Well, how could the ancient Mayans be praying to the Christian God? The gods they prayed to, with their beliefs, demanded human sacrifice."

"Where are you going with this?" interjected Bobby.

"People are screwed up, man. We want to believe what we want to believe, regardless of whether it's right or not. It's moral relativism—the idea that there is no such thing as objective truth," I stated in a nutshell.

"I don't think it's as black and white as that," answered Bobby.

"That's the problem."

"What?" Jimmy replied, setting us on the path toward a "Who's on first" conundrum.

"What you are saying is that it's impossible to know the difference between good and evil," I clarified. "Look at Hitler for example. Do you think Hitler shares the same fate as a Carmelite nun? If that's the case, what's the point of being good or doing charitable works? It's all for nothing."

"That's not true. You do it because it's the right thing to do. It's self-evident," Jimmy theorized.

"Maybe if you're an Ayn Rand objectivist," I joked. "What makes it right? Is it right because you say it's right? My point is, it's right because there is a difference between good and evil, and we've got to get that clarification from God. Otherwise, where does truth come from? Thin air? We can't get that clarification from humans, because humans all have different beliefs and different perceptions of reality."

"I think you can get that from a majority opinion. If most people know it's right, then it should be taken as being right. We live in a democracy, and with good reason," asserted Jimmy, as though our form of government had anything to do with the discussion.

"Actually, we live in a republic, jackass, not a democracy," I corrected condescendingly. "Ever recite the Pledge of Allegiance?"

"Whatever, dude."

"But either way, let's use your example. If a popular majority thinks slavery is justifiable, does that make it right? Or genocide, does that make it right?" I asked.

"There's also natural law, T. People aren't going to vote for genocide."

"Fair enough, but what about abortion?"

Jimmy once again changed the subject, proclaiming, "Look, I don't think God wants people to be miserable, and I think that's the problem with organized religion in general. It's the rules and restrictions that start making people insane."

I got the sense that Jimmy was looking for a "way out"—some theological rationale that would eliminate any Catholic guilt.

"Look, I don't think God wants people to be miserable either, but when you have little children, are you going to let them play in a busy street just because they want the freedom to do so? No way, right? You gonna let them eat twelve Snickers bars before bed? The rules you impose keep them safe, and keep them happy. You gotta ask, is monogamy a restriction, or is it a prerequisite for happy married life?"

Johnny offered no response, so he simply made a face as if to say, "Yeah. Maybe. Whatever."

"Let's take homosexuals, like Bobby for example," I said, taunting my roommate. "Either homosexual activity is justifiable in the eyes of God, or it's offensive to Him; same thing with abortion. There is no in-between. You have to hold a position one way or the other. You guys have to agree with me on that."

"But how can you possibly know what God believes?" asked Bobby, with a puzzled look on his face.

"See, I think God wants us to know the truth. I don't see why God would create us otherwise," I replied.

"I got one for you, T," replied Jimmy, as he prepared a trump card of his own. "Why did God create evil? I have a hard time believing in a God that sits back and watches a fifteen-year-old girl get raped, or a tiny kid die of hunger in Africa. You're gonna tell me there's a good God sittin' back with his popcorn watching that go on and not doing something about it? Gimme a break. The more I think about it, God is Santa Claus. He's a nice thought. You say God loves us and He wants to be loved. Go snap a picture of a malnourished infant with flies on his face begging for a handout from Sally Struthers and tell me God loves us."

"Well, I don't know man," I said. "I don't think that's what God had in mind at the outset."

"Tell that to the infant," he said, as he stood up to leave. "Man, it's all one crazy mess. I need to crash, boys. Good chattin'. Yo T— do us all a favor and don't go turnin' into Billy Graham, alright?"

Bobby and I washed up and shut off the lights. The noise in the hallway faded, and the dorm settled down for its late night recharge. My mind quickly entered into a half-asleep, half-awake zone, and I began thinking about Jimmy's argument. I thought of a dozen different comebacks and things I should have said to him, until I realized that none of them were particularly convincing. Then I began to wonder myself: *Maybe he's right. Why does God allow so much nastiness in the world? Why doesn't He do something about it if He loves us so much? Maybe God IS Santa Claus.*

The next morning I rose to my normal routine, but I felt unmistakably different. Though I couldn't pinpoint the catalyst for the change, the thought of further exploring my spirituality suddenly seemed nonsensical. In the span of one night's sleep, I winced at the notion of offering a morning prayer to God. Perhaps this sudden one-eighty was caused by the doubt that festered in my REM state, or perhaps my internal window for spiritual soul-searching had closed. No one can maintain that level of serious introspection forever, I figured. Either way, it was as though the cloud of spirituality in which I had immersed myself for over a week had been lifted, and it happened quickly. It was similar to the feeling of being lost in a movie theater during a long, three-hour film, where you feel transported into a different world for what seems like a lifetime before the credits roll and the bright daylight awakens you to reality. By morning I had come down from my spiritual high, and I began sensing a renewed excitement for the weekend. Subconsciously my spiritual mood reverted back to its old, regular self.

My buddies welcomed the return of their prodigal son with open arms and bottles of champagne (Miller High Life, the champagne of beers). In truth, no one had any insight into my struggles, but they knew I had taken a couple nights off from boozing. My return to reality couldn't have been more timely, as St. Patrick's Day in New Hampshire is no time for religious conviction. During the course of the next three weeks it was beer pong and phone numbers, video games and working out, March

Madness and Spring Break. It was the same old college carousel. As spring blossomed on our college campus, everything seemed normal as ever until 3:30 AM one Saturday.

I strolled into the bathroom of my wing after a very long night of drinking, and the room was unnaturally clean with the overwhelming smell of disinfectant. As I passed by a mirror above one of the sinks, I paused, turned, and stared into my reflection for several moments. Then I laughed at myself, and laughed some more at myself laughing. I thought to myself how crazy I looked, and I became angry and embarrassed. Then I became depressed. In my head I spoke to God: *It is You who made me like this. It is You who made the world like this.*

The ups and downs of my faith in college were steep and frequent. The very next day I was miserable again, and I began rehashing the same spiritual arguments as before, once again beginning with the problem: *Is there a God?* Eventually, I ended up back at Jimmy's stumbling block question, which continued to bother me, and in time I decided to challenge someone who might offer a compelling response.

I brought the issue to one of the monks at my Benedictine college, Father Albert, who moonlighted as my Humanities professor. He was a short and rotund man with a hearty laugh and a genial personality, and he was a favorite among students although he was a harsh grader. I stopped him one afternoon on his way through the quad and I asked if I could ask him a question, to which he nodded, "Certainly!"

"If God is so good, why did he create evil, father?"

A warm and holy man, he appreciated the genuine skepticism in my voice, and he approached my question with the simplicity and conviction of a man who had devoted his life to the topic.

"Ah, the problem of evil! That's a tough one, isn't it, Mr.

Saab?" he laughed.

"Yes, father. I can't wrap my mind around it. I've been thinking about it a lot."

"Well, what is evil, son? Let us start with that question, okay?
St. Augustine in his *Confessions* explains evil this way: he says
that evil, as a thing, does not actually exist, you see, because
evil is a term used to describe a deficiency in *goodness*. Understand? If you bought a whole pizza and it came with only one
slice, that pizza would be deficient because it is missing the other
seven slices. Where goodness is not perfect, that is what we call
evil. In other words, good is *something*, evil is *something missing*.
Therefore, good and evil can be more accurately stated as good
and 'not good.'"

"Okay, I follow you, father."

"Walk with me," he commanded. "God only created good,
you see. So Mr. Saab, your question really is this: why does God
allow good to be missing in the world, is it not?" he asked.

"I guess so, father."

"Okay. Well why did God create the world in the first place?"
he asked rhetorically. "God created the world because He desires
that we share in His perfect love, you see. It is really that simple.
In order for this perfect love to exist, it requires that He bestow
upon man the gift of free will, giving us the option of loving
Him. How can there be true love if we are forced to love Him?
Love without free will is nothing! Imagine if a person forced you
unwillingly to love a woman off of the street—we wouldn't call
that a relationship at all, would we, let alone the foundation for
a covenant? God endows us with the ability to reject Him, and
this rejection is what evil is, you see. Evil is choice. Sometimes it
is a direct choice, but very often an indirect one. That's why it's
important for us, as Christians, to rid not only ourselves of evil,

but the whole world of evil as well."

"I understand father, thank you."

"Does this answer your question?"

"Well, kind of. What about suffering? What about a tiny baby in Africa who has no food? Is that his choice? He's innocent, isn't he?"

"He is suffering because of another man's evil. He is suffering because of a tyrannical government that controls the food supply," he replied. "But to your point, let's take another example. Let us say someone is suffering because of a natural disaster, an earthquake or something. Now you might argue there is no evil involved at all, correct?"

"Sure," I nodded.

"Well, suffering in general is a very difficult concept for us. To suffer, it would seem, is the greatest human fear. Theologically, we would say that suffering entered the world the moment evil entered the world, and is therefore a byproduct of evil, you see. But the glory of the Passion is that suffering can be made into something beautiful."

"But I thought that was the point of the crucifixion. Didn't Christ take our sins upon Himself? Why would God want us to suffer?"

"God wants us to *love*, Mr. Saab. To LOVE! You see? I will ask you, then: can there be love without suffering? Can there be love without sacrifice??"

"Without sacrifice, no. But suffering?"

"We can turn our suffering into a gift, son. A gift to God. We can offer up our pain to God and bear it nobly, and pray that our sacrifice might appease the sorrows committed *against* His love. Do you understand?" he asked. "Why did Christ suffer and die for us?"

"To save our souls."

"Ah, but He is God, He is *infinite* Goodness. One tiny, miniscule drop of His blood would have been enough to save all of mankind for eternity," he explained, squeezing his thumb and his index finger together. "So why did He suffer and die the most horrible death imaginable?"

"To be an example?" I guessed.

"Precisely! *Precisely.* Now you understand. He offers us the most perfect example of love. Eleven of the twelve apostles—now I'm including Judas' replacement Mathias here as well—they followed Christ's example and they all suffered and died terribly out of love! You see? Only John averted a martyr's death, and you might say that his suffering came at the foot of the cross. The early Christians, a good many of them suffered and died horrifically out of love. In fact, the Roman Coliseum was irrigated by Christian blood. Do you see? We are not all called to be martyrs, to be sure, but we are all called to love God with that same passion and zeal, with that same urgency. The suffering we bear should be offered up to God as a wonderful gift of love, my boy. If you only knew! Suffering can be transformed into something so very, very beautiful!"

Father Albert's explanation was unlike anything I had heard before.

"Do you have that strength inside you, party boy?" he asked paternally, driving his index finger into my chest.

"I don't think so father. Not yet," I replied humbly.

"Honesty! Good man, never lie to your priest. Consider what I've told you, okay?" he smiled, and gave me a blessing before shuffling away.

Father Albert's profound understanding of the faith was magnetic and inspiring to me. He was the type of man I would follow into battle though he was the antithesis of a warrior. I couldn't help but wonder what other impossible riddles he had solved and stored in his oversized dome. One thing was certain: his views didn't jibe with my lifestyle, and if I followed my inclination to embrace them, I was setting myself up to be a hypocrite or a pariah. Conforming my actions to my beliefs would force a monumental social change.

Despite my aversion to such a change, I found myself sculpting in my head a vision of the man I wanted to be, if for no other reason than to create an ideal for comparison's sake. The quintessential me was far removed from the ideals of the modern-day everyman; instead he resembled a gentlemanly crossbreed between Clark Kent and, well . . . Charlemagne. I even scribbled these character traits on an oversized Post-It note and hid it inside my desk. It read:

The man I want to be . . .

- *Prays*, recognizing that his duty is to God first above all things.

- Is *articulate*, communicating his thoughts and opinions intelligently and respectfully.

- *Respects women*, directly, through honorable discourse and chaste living, and indirectly, by his thoughts.

- *Defends the innocent*, especially children and unborn life.

- Is *not addicted*—whether to alcohol, pornography, or entertainment—and therefore truly free.

- Is *healthy*, actively maintaining physical fitness and a proper diet.

- Holds *convictions* supported by reason and truth.

- Is *courageous*, unafraid to defend truth in all circumstances.

- *Educates* himself, not for the sake of accumulating factual knowledge, but for advancement in wisdom.

- *Works hard*, acknowledging that time is a gift to be used wisely.
- *Sacrifices* his needs for the sake of others.
- Is *charitable*, recognizing that nothing is truly his own.
- Is *humble*, possessing an honesty that doesn't tolerate deception, and a gratitude without envy.

In reality, I was a chalk outline of that man, a jagged image without an identity. I was elusive and enigmatic, indulging in the artificial highs of living without the anchor of truth, while still attempting to front as someone noble. I feared the jeers of my friends and a life within the boundaries of staunch principles. Further still, abandoning the excitement of college-life was an undesirable prospect, and it demoralized my honorable intentions. While my friends were lapping up the thrills of Friday-night partying, I couldn't resign myself to playing pinochle and Yahtzee at the local vfw. The distance to where I wanted to go seemed too great, and I lacked the moxie to make the leap. I loved what I hated, and hated that I loved it.

An interior tug-of-war for my soul had begun. I had laid down the gauntlet of manhood, but felt ill prepared for the difficulty or gravity of the battle. My enemies concealed themselves in attractive masks, from the riches of the world to the temptations of women to my entertainment-filled addictions. Ironically, they were the least of my worries. My greatest enemy was myself.

part two

five

a boy in a business suit

I WOULD LOVE TO TELL YOU that "The List" transformed me, and, energized by my newfound wisdom, I confronted the world as a changed, honorable man—but it just didn't happen that way. I'm not entirely sure why I couldn't make the transition. Perhaps in a different time or a different place, surrounded by strong support in an environment fertilized by virtue, my mustard seed of conviction would have taken root. But before long the quicksand of college life sucked me down, and in my weakness, I buried that list. In every ensuing moment of despair, after a night of binge-drinking or an uncomfortable hook-up, it was as though a devilish Jack Nicholson would perch himself on my shoulder and sneer, *"You can't handle the truth!"* It's one thing for a person to live his life as a vacuous shell without fully comprehending the extent of his transgressions, but I was guilty of the greater sin; I knew what was right, and I chose to reject it.

Loneliness was the big culprit. I had plenty of friends, but I lacked companionship. I could never keep a girlfriend, because

I couldn't find any girls who wanted the guy I wanted to be—at least none that I was attracted to. I hated the idea of dating anyone less than my soul mate for an extended period of time. It just seemed too superficial, and I couldn't keep the ruse going for very long. It was like renting companionship. It was an investment that depreciated in value. By dating someone I knew I would never marry, I figured I just set myself up for a painful breakup, and I placed a barrier between the potential girl of my dreams and me. You can't meet new people when you are out on a date.

My response was to dive deeper into a greater fantasy, fabricating the feeling of companionship by getting drunk and "hooking up," without the commitment or the emotional investment. Of course, I was just making it harder on myself, because temporary moments of pleasure never lead to lasting fulfillment. It's like when someone eats a pack of Twinkies when they're depressed about being overweight—the pleasure adds to the problem. Strangely, the reins of faith always seemed to hold fast when I was on the verge of taking a good time over the edge, as though even in my worst moments a glimmer of hope remained. I continued glancing toward the future, daydreaming about how life would be different once I hit the working world and established myself. I figured change was the catalyst I needed to burst out of my funk, but in the meantime I decided to continue sowing my wild oats while I had an excuse.

Ironically, I coped with the guilt of my behavior by revving up the good works. If I couldn't correct the destructive behavior, I thought, I would balance it out with as many good works as possible. As I grew into an upperclassman, I became more comfortable and sociable with other groups on campus and less concerned with my image. I had developed so much history with my friends that damaging those bonds became unlikely, and it freed me to fraternize with others without putting up a front. These new relationships allowed me to explore aspects of my character that I concealed from most people. I began spending my college breaks volunteering for the less privileged. I created better friendships with Randy and the other kids involved with Campus Ministry, and I enjoyed their company. I even began organizing and leading retreats. I drove to orphanages and played games with little children, held mother-less infants, and I mentored an eleven-year-old kid I called my little brother. My interest in religious activities intensified and I attended Mass regularly, sometimes even more than once per week. As a senior, I worked aggressively to instruct the freshmen not to fall into the same pitfalls I had. When I was good, I was really good, but I struggled to stay fully committed despite how much I enjoyed it all. Rather than changing my lifestyle entirely, I compartmentalized it, allowing each group of friends to encounter one aspect of my personality. I did not want to place restrictions on my behavior; I wanted to live all lifestyles because no one way of life satisfied me entirely. My college years were plagued by contradiction.

—

SIX MONTHS BEFORE GRADUATION I accepted a job offer in Sales and Marketing at a Fortune 500 tech company in Dallas. I would ultimately finish college with two degrees, one in Liberal Arts and the other in Electrical Engineering, but I was never a bookworm, and I certainly did not leave behind a legacy of academic achievement. I decided to pursue an engineering degree for the practicality of it—the job security and the potential for upper-middle class money. As such, I never saw much value in a 4.0 GPA except for the pride of accomplishment. To me, it was the equivalent of beating Super Mario Brothers on the original Nintendo—it takes some talent and plenty of time, but ultimately means very little. Instead, I focused most of my attention on student leadership, relationships, and social networking. I knew I could pick up the rest rather easily.

Even though my grades were never stellar, I always interviewed well, and as fortune would have it, the tech boom in 1999 and 2000 created a fierce demand for talent in electrical and computer engineering. After a series of mundane and highly analytical summer internships, I interviewed for positions in technical sales and marketing to bridge the gap between my degree and my interests. Executives were always caught off-guard by my honesty, because it humanized me in a way that made me stand out from the generic, inflated ramblings of other prospects.

Executive #1: Tarek, your resume looks strong, but it's not perfect. I have a list of resumes here that stack up pretty well with yours, if not better, especially with regards to GPA. If you had one thing to do over again in, say, the last ten years, what would it be?

Me: Well, I was a real a—hole to my mother when I was fifteen. If I could do anything over again it would be to treat her like she deserved to be treated.

Executive #1: Wow, I must say I've never heard that one before, but I appreciate the honesty. I have a fifteen-year old son myself, and my wife and I are dealing with some of that right now. Any advice?

Me: How much time do we have?

Executive #2: Tarek, I've done probably ten interviews today, and my favorite question to ask the candidates is: "What are your career aspirations?" Everyone says they want to be an executive, but there are only so many executives in this company. Do you think you are executive material?

Me: So . . . would you like to know my career aspirations or if I'm executive material?

Executive #2: Let's start with career aspirations.

Me: I want to own a stud farm of Arabian horses on a couple hundred acres of land, and I want to breed and sell them. I'm a city kid who dreams of the country.

Executive #2: [chuckling] Are you serious? A stud farm?

Me: [smiling] Very serious.

Executive #2: Why?

Me: I used to ride horses. They're amazing creatures, and I've always had a desire for land and property. I think there is something very real and virile about it, but I recognize that it will take time and money. The road to paradise runs through the corporate world for me. I won't get what I want unless I make you and this company a lot of money.

Executive #2: Okay, I appreciate that. I think we all have dreams like that. Do you think you're executive material?

Me: Well, I guess that just depends. In many places, being promoted to an executive position has nothing to do with ability or past performance; it's about longevity and looking the part and knowing the right people and using phrases like "thinking outside the box" and "peeling back the onion." Is this company like that? Or is this the type of place that promotes its shining stars into positions of leadership? If it is the former, then I'll never be an executive here. There are ten other *nice* candidates with *nice* resumes from *nice* schools that will fit into the standard mold. If it's the latter, and the company is focused on winning and wiping the mat with the competition, then I'll be running one of your divisions by the time I'm thirty.

Executive #2: [smiling] Well, you certainly don't lack confidence!

Me: Can you lack confidence and be executive material?

I had four job offers by December of my senior year, and I accepted the dream package for any twenty-two-year-old with a standard bachelor's degree: $60,000 base salary, $10,000 signing bonus, $6,000 relocation package, one-thousand stock options, $600 per month car allowance, sales bonuses up to 20 percent of my base salary, three weeks paid vacation, a matching 401K plan plus additional 2 percent company adder, etc. It was more than the yearly salary of both of my parents. The hallmarks of my adolescent vision of success—a good salary and job security—became a reality for me five months before I had even graduated from college.

Ecstatic about the forthcoming prosperity, I leveraged my offer letter into securing a loan for my first car; a brand new 2001 fully loaded Nissan Pathfinder. I purchased it on Valentine's Day; a 240 horsepower, 4x4, black-leather-interior-sun-roofed-gadget-bedecked-power-everything dream ride. I proceeded to parade it around campus all spring, bling-blingin' as though I'd finally achieved something. In May 2001, after five enigmatic years, I received my passport to job-worthiness, and I confronted the real world, a boy in a business suit.

The two thousand mile trek from Boston to Dallas, from the quaint cottages of New England, through the winding roads of the Blue Ridge Mountains towards the dry simplicity of Texas, was a music-laden journey that was characteristically Cameron Crowe. With my TripTik and sunflower seeds I motored along to a soundtrack of U2, Bob Seger, and Pat Green, as my mind continually lapsed into long hours of deep self-reflection. The trip was a metamorphosis of sorts. Just as when Lucy walked through the wardrobe into Narnia, the journey had little to do with distance and more to do with my state of mind. As much as I had been ready to finish school and leave parental protection and menial jobs, I was mostly looking forward to my transfiguration into manhood. A man has his own place and cash to burn. He has health and dental insurance and owns dress pants, and he wears a watch that costs more than fifty dollars. A man knows the difference between cabernet and merlot, he pays full price for a movie, and he listens to talk radio. A man is respected.

In what seemed like an instant, three weeks removed from my last college class, I found myself in another classroom, but this time I excitedly lapped up the Kool-aid of my corporate orientation, wagging my tail like an enthusiastic puppy and eager to sprint on the fast track to white-collar nirvana. This time it mattered. It was like transitioning from the practice field to the game field. I envisioned myself as a young Gordon Gecko with designs on Wall Street. I went to the men's store and bought three more business suits, even though the dress code was business casual. I walked differently, and I spoke differently, and I soon made a name for myself as an up-and-comer within the cluttered class system of corporate society. I felt empowered by my paycheck and my position, and I embraced my career with the excitement of knowing that the future had finally arrived.

The newness and the routine of my budding career became intoxicating, and the spiritual fascination of my college years began to disintegrate in turn. I loved work and the competitive challenge tied to it. It was like a nine-hour contest every day. My apartment was 9.3 miles from the office, and my normal route sometimes included a stop at the dry cleaners—*extra starch please*—or the car wash—*you missed a spot*. I even began drinking coffee, because every professional drinks coffee, and each morning at 8:00 AM I'd pop into the shop to buy a steaming cup of corporate goodness. For the first time in a long time I had a sense of who I was—I was a businessman—and I conformed everything I did around that image.

Not surprisingly, the polish and formality wore off little by little, and my masquerade of maturity was revealed before long. Beneath the austere formalities of business cards and titles, I began to discover a very familiar subculture, as the other new college hires in the exclusive program attempted to stamp their place as the alpha dog of good times. It made sense, because outside of the office we had nothing else to do, so we clung together in a sort of professional fraternity. In a matter of months, I came to the disturbing realization that I hadn't left my past behind at all. The real man beneath the half-Windsor eventually resurfaced, where rigidity loosened to swagger, and my dull version of Bruce Banner morphed into the party Hulk. Though my days were entrenched in "TPS" reports and Microsoft Excel, my nights were filled inhaling 75-cent rail drinks at the club Happy Hour. I wasn't an alcoholic; I was a *sociaholic*, rapidly assuming the role of captain on the ship of making friends and blowing money. After all, it was a natural place for me, I figured; I was a wise-ass with a 2.8 GPA. I hadn't been an honor student since high school.

Admittedly, my peer group was an eclectic cast of characters, a mix of frat boys and Class A wannabes. Some were the nerdy type, geeked up by the fact that their elevated salary placed them in a class above the cool crowd they once idolized, and unclear about what to do with their free time without a test or report to prepare for. Others were surprisingly unmotivated, satisfied that they'd already achieved their goal of gainful employment. Then there were the hybrids; otherwise normal guys who were immediately discontented with their jobs and who had already earmarked business school as the stepping-stone to their professional aspirations (which were strictly related to wealth generation). The women, rare in the engineering world, mainly fell into three stereotypes: beautiful airheads with a penchant for sleeping around, degree hunters validated by paper progress, or twenty-something versions of Thelma Harper from *Mama's Family*.

Nevertheless, we were all connected through our company, and still mired in that strange purgatory between adolescence and adulthood, not really knowing how to act, not developing lasting friendships, and perpetually dreaming of bigger things. We were essentially college kids with a professional budget, but this time there was no Campus Ministry, no Fr. Albert, and no sense of mystery beyond the confines of our industrial home. As a result, I boarded up the side of my personality that conflicted with my surroundings. I still made an effort to attend church weekly, but it became a check mark on my list of errands. The business world had become my new place of worship, where I sought an end to my search for satisfaction. Surrounding all the activity, behind the Express button down shirts and Banana Republic flat-front pants and outwardly sanguine disposition, was a universal sense of post-college uncertainty—about life, about love, and about happiness.

Unlike college, the late nights did not affect my job performance negatively; they enhanced it. I assumed the mantle of leadership within our office because I was a leader outside of it, and I brought a certain edginess to the workplace that few, if any, had the courage to bring. It hadn't taken long for the real me to break through the starch—an overconfident, insecure, intelligent, confused, articulate, driven *boy*. My goals were simple; I wanted to manage people, to direct, to stake my claim as the proverbial big fish in the little pond, though I quickly learned that looking the part was safe but unimpressive. The more I loosened up and hee-hawed with management the more they respected me. As the saying went, success was never about what you knew; it was about *who* you knew, about relationships with people.

In a short time, I'd received rave reviews from my boss, my boss's boss, and my boss's boss's boss. Each additional "boss" was like a gold star in elementary school, and I racked them up like perfect attendance stickers in the second grade, when I sported v-neck sweaters and penny loafers and had a crush on my teacher despite her puritanical outfits. The competitive rat race didn't suck me in; I dove in head-first, but what I sought was more than a pat on the back or an "attaboy," it was validation of a different kind, as though my sense of self-worth was tied exclusively to my job and my paycheck. I desired respect from more than just the company hierarchy; beneath a happy-go-lucky smile I wanted my peers and co-workers to admire me. A psychologist would have a field day with the reasons why, but at its heart it was a struggle to find purpose. Without the necessary humility to worship, I subconsciously desired to *be* worshipped, not in a crazy Napoleonic manner, but like a modern-day celebrity. Whenever

I felt slightly unfulfilled, I pressed the gas pedal harder in all directions, thinking that perhaps I would discover that magic something a little further along into the future.

Management enjoyed having me around because I would help them call to mind the "glory days" of their bachelorhood. I would get invitations to exclusive sushi dinners with Japanese executives, where I'd observe how middle-aged, mid-level managers would select everything off the menu, order endless rounds of booze, laugh heartily at eighth-grade jokes, toast to prosperity and comment crudely on the Texas-bred waitresses. Nobody paid for anything themselves. They discussed Range Rovers and BMWs, five-thousand-square-foot mansions, golf trips to Florida, and their wives' unchecked spending habits. I'd been introduced to an entirely different world, and I loved the new boys club and the feeling of assurance that came with it. For the first time, I felt like somebody—somebody important. The fraternizing led to mentorship, and I became the guy they wanted me to be, the up-and-comer on the fast track.

I also abandoned "my list." I couldn't reconcile it with the attraction of my new career. You don't bring an identity into Corporate America. An identity is given to you, one that is defined by conformity. My job wasn't simply a part of my world; my job was my world:

> Such and such are the company priorities.
>
> Such and such is the company mission.
>
> Such and such are the company values.

The machine assimilated me, and my faith in God evaporated faster than I could say "money."

corporate dreamscape

THE BLISTERING TEXAS SUMMER gave way to an unseasonably mild, overcast day in early September, and as I stood in the coffee area pouring my second cup of the morning, I felt altogether lethargic. Even the simplest movements required abnormal effort, like in one of those dreams when your body won't cooperate with normal exercises. My eyes hung low. For three months I'd floated to new heights in my quest toward corporate satisfaction, but on this day, ironically, with a schedule devoid of any meetings or lunch plans or seminars, I felt inescapably trapped in the reality of mundane jobhood. As I flipped through the calendar in my drab, monochromatic cubicle, I reflected on the fact that this was my first September away from school in seventeen years. They say graduation is the first day of the rest of your life, but that really isn't true. Graduation is just the beginning of summer, and Labor Day is the beginning of the rest of your life.

"Tarek! What's up bud? Crazy night last night?" asked Ralph, one of the managers in my department, shortly after I'd reached my office.

"Nah, it was slow," I replied, burning my mouth on my molten-hot joe.

"Listen, reports are due today, so I'm going to need you to run your numbers. Make sure you divide the PT by CBD on chart four, and if the FIC looks high, it's probably because our quarterly SPQ is off. Convert it into PDF, don't send an Excel file. Also, would you mind running these documents down to B-Wing, and can you please tell Sarah to proof read her e-mails before she sends them to customers? She spells like Corky, and her cute little ass won't cover up her mistakes over e-mail," he explained, whispering the last half of the sentence with a wry smile.

"Corky had Down syndrome, he wasn't dyslexic," I clarified, rising to Corky's defense.

"Well, whatever. By 4:00 PM, okay?"

"Sure, no problem," I grinned, restraining what I really wanted to say to him. Truth be told, though the acronyms were a mouthful at times and the reports appeared to be complex, my work demanded little cognitive ability. It baffled me that they hired some of the brightest minds in the country to be paper pushers. My job began to reflect the office stereotypes comedically spotlighted in Office Space and Dilbert, and each day I would notice it with greater regularity.

"Hey, by the way, what did you think of the presentation yesterday?" he continued, seeking approval for his artsy PowerPoint demo, forgetting that I had already commented on it during the meeting.

"Well, like I mentioned yesterday, I just don't think the strategy will work. Offering nominal incentives to distributors won't do enough to change practice. People move when something important is at stake. If you offered me free lunch to run my reports, I wouldn't be motivated to do it. If you threatened to dock my pay, then you'd have my attention. We're a top-three supplier for them, so tell them we'll pull some accounts unless they get their act together. Spare the rod, spoil the child," I stated, capping my rant with the requisite cliché.

"Well, we'll see. We've spent a long time on this, so we're not going to just change directions now."

"Even if you know it won't work?"

"It doesn't work that way around here," he concluded, while tapping my office wall twice out of awkwardness, and making a face as if to say don't press the issue before rushing off.

I sat deeply in my chair and crossed my hands, gazing vacantly into the computer screen. My conversation with Ralph was eerily typical, and it was just another crack in the shell of optimism that, for three months, had surrounded me. This wasn't nirvana. In many cases a rational argument would fall on deaf ears; other times, a harmless word might incur the wrath of the human resources department. I was once told to remove a Red Sox poster because a Yankees fan in the office "didn't appreciate it." They were training the real me to be an automaton, which I embraced at first, until I realized I yearned to be a free spirit. I felt a real sense of disillusionment as I peered intently into my computer screen, my window to the world in a window-less office. I reminisced about the "life-long" college friends who I'd already lost touch with, and I felt claustrophobic. The fluorescent lights above illuminated the new dawn of my life, and I sat there brooding, a high-paid lab rat in a cubicle maze.

For a brief moment, a spark of faith ignited a thought towards heavenly things, as though the promise of happiness led somewhere far different than my present situation, but it seemed too mystical to grasp. I dreamt about more tangible pleasures, like a BMW; not a 3-series like the rich girls drive, but a 5-series, the director's car, the *man's* ride. I pictured myself in control of the tight suspension and smooth power, with its bucket seats and sharp acoustics and . . ."What am I doing?" I thought, as reason interrupted the fantasy. "I just bought a brand-new, $35,000 car a few months ago."

I recoiled back in my chair, and burned my mouth once again on my blistering coffee. I thought, was I really nesting into the next forty years of my life? Was this the vision of the man I wanted to be? Am I really climbing towards the pinnacle of earthly contentment? I had been toeing the line between worldly stimulation and the ever-increasing weight of my conscience, and now I felt myself plunging into the autumn of my discontent, allowing honesty for the first time to unmask the rose-colored lenses of my corporate dreamscape. I thought about anything that might offer fulfillment—beautiful girls, a high-ranking executive position, a farm of Arabian horses, a movie deal, a professional sports contract, fame, and on and on. Some of those things were simply unrealistic, and others were flat out impossibilities. I also considered other jobs, but nothing jumped out at me, in part because I was unsure of myself, and also because I couldn't claim any recognizable talents other than talking—and I wasn't sure that was even a talent. I felt so one-dimensional, so unaccomplished.

During my first week in college, Fr. Albert stated, "One of the marks of an educated man is to know a little about everything and a lot about *something*." That statement struck a chord with me. I've always been in awe of a gifted musician, or a master craftsman, or an expert scientist, people who are known to be unrivaled in a particular field. Their talent places a firm stamp on their identity: "This is Bill, he's an outstanding tailor" or "Jim plays a mean viola" or whatever. I was envious of their opportunity to work with their hands, and to retire each night with a sense of singular accomplishment. A furniture maker witnesses the daily progression of his table or bureau and departs from his work with great satisfaction. A pianist might go home upon mastering a new work and feel the rush of achieving a personal milestone. I wondered if it was that type of hands-on mastery I needed for self-satisfaction.

My identity was far more ambiguous. I owned none of my tasks autonomously, yet still maintained responsibility for the large-scale outcome of broad departmental initiatives. Being a "team player" is only fun when your team is good. When the team is riddled with corporate totem poles, the experience becomes defeating. Since nothing was entirely my own, my personal objectives related not to the business; instead, they concerned only salary and promotion. Without some sort of daily management endorsement, measuring personal progress was a nearly impossible task. In time, the work, the strategies, the goals—they mattered only to the extent that in fulfilling my specific obligations I might be recognized and rewarded. On certain evenings I would drive home after a long day mired in e-mail correspondence with customers and colleagues and wonder: what did I really accomplish, and for whom did I accomplish it? In reality, I was a corporate mercenary, employee number J01-93374, and the money didn't even satisfy me.

Shortly after Ralph left my office, I received a phone call from my manager, Dan, to whom I reported directly. Dan was thirty-four and also from New England, and we had built up a pretty strong rapport given our mutual interest in the Boston sports scene. As a result, our meetings were typically informal.

"Tarek, can I see you in my office?" he commanded.

"Uh, Sure." I swung around the corner to the other side of the wall and poked my head in the door.

"Sit down, man" he began. "How are you doing?"

"I'm fine."

"Are you?" he asked.

"Yeah, why? What's up? Am I in trouble or something?" I asked.

"Haha! No, no, no," he laughed. "Not in trouble. It's just that some people have mentioned that you've been a little curt in meetings recently."

"Was there something specific?" I asked, well aware of what he was referring to.

"No, no, not something specific," he replied in defense. "It's just that I think sometimes you can come across as being a little insensitive with people."

"Okay," I said, staring at him blankly. He expected an apology or at least a response of some kind, but I didn't offer one. Instead I let the silence escalate, forcing him to fumble through the uncomfortable reprimand. I liked him, but I didn't like being scolded.

"So . . . will you try to be more sensitive?" he asked.

"Unless you can give me an example of what you want me to correct, how do I know what I'm correcting?" I asked, being more difficult than I needed to be.

"C'mon, man. You know what I'm talking about," he replied impatiently. "You told Ralph in his meeting that his idea was *stupid*."

"It is."

"You can make your point without using the word 'stupid'. Just say you have a better suggestion or something. You know what I mean."

"Are we in kindergarten?"

"Just use a different word, okay? You're doing amazing here. Everyone has you pegged as a superstar. Just be a little less sharp."

I shook my head and peered downward.

"C'mon," he urged.

"Alright," I nodded reluctantly, withholding my frustration.

I returned to my desk, but I wanted to get out of there. I didn't want to open up Excel, I didn't want to think about SPQ, and I didn't want to speak to anyone else. My job was making me feel nothing like a real man. Throughout the course of human existence the defining characteristic of manhood has been physical strength. In the most primal sense, I began craving a more rugged, or at least tactile, expression of my manhood. The stationary nature of my job was consigning my body to a physical state of atrophy—unless I worked-out in addition to work. My co-workers were marshmallows, and I cringed at the future vision of myself as a lard-carrying forty-year-old, let alone a domesticated one. It wasn't about summoning my inner Paul Bunyon, I simply felt emasculated by my inability to build a fire or shoot a rifle. Even the academics in the olden days, the professors and doctors and politicians, maintained some connection to the land through hunting and chopping firewood and the like. In his book *Wild at Heart*, John Eldredge unravels this problem best:

> The way a man's life unfolds nowadays tends to drive his heart into remote regions of his soul. Endless hours at a computer screen; selling shoes at the mall; meetings, memos, phone calls. The business world—where the majority of American men live and die—requires a man to be efficient and punctual. Corporate policies and procedures are designed with one aim: to harness a man to the plow and make

him produce. But the soul refuses to be harnessed; it knows nothing of Day Timers and deadlines and P&L statements. The soul longs for passion, for freedom, for *life* . . . A man needs to feel the rhythms of the earth; he needs to have in hand something real—the tiller of a boat, a set of reins, the roughness of rope, or simply a shovel. Can a man live all his days to keep his fingernails clean and trim?

But I came out of my daze and acknowledged that I had it pretty damn good, of course. With high earnings potential and numerous benefits, the company provided far more than what I'd earned. I had a great job. There were plenty of farmers who would have relished the opportunity to sit on their rear end all day and make an honest wage. It would take an inflated sense of entitlement and extreme ingratitude to cast aside all of my good fortune to become a shepherd or something. Even most other professionals, let alone college grads, would have killed for my job. Defecting in order to pursue other ambitions as a starving artist or a lumberjack was far from an appealing proposition. I decided to focus my energy on something other than alternative employment, thinking maybe I was missing the big picture.

"T, we're doing happy hour tonight after work at Chuy's. You in?" asked Rajeev, interrupting my pity party. Rajeev had come into the program right around the same time I had and worked in a nearby office.

"Yeah, I'm in for sure. I need a beer," I nodded.

"Work hard, play hard, baby!" he replied in his Indian accent.

"Hey, Jackson mentioned something about putting together a flag football team. Is that plan still in the works?" I asked.

"As far as I know. By the way, Jason and Will wanted me to tell you they are having a *Halo* tournament tonight if you want to come," he said, referring to the video game.

"On a Friday night? What are we, fourteen? They know I'm not into that."

"Hey, gaming is big business, man," he chuckled. "I just read this article in *BusinessWeek* that said 40 percent of gamers are adults. We're not talking about Pac-man and Donkey Kong anymore."

"That's unbelievable."

"You could just come and hang out. What else are you going to do?"

"I don't know. Not that."

I chose not to purchase a television (let alone video games) when I moved to Dallas, partly because I never got around to it and partly because I held the principle that life without a television was in itself a virtuous act. I considered TV to be a slothful distraction, but while removing the tube may have eliminated the slothful, it certainly didn't eliminate the distractions. I masked my anxieties by living a crowded and event-filled life outside of work, diverting my attention to other forms of entertainment.

The intramural football and basketball leagues at the apartment complex and the company gym promised some combination of "fun, exercise, and excitement," and I participated in every league, expanding my network of acquaintances to such a degree that I always had a party to attend or a golf outing on the calendar. Weight lifting became a central priority, and I woke up every morning at 5:30 AM for my workout, not because it was an ideal time to exercise, but because I wanted to start my day doing something for *me*. An inner addiction drove me to be leaner and stronger, and I supplemented my chicken breast and shake diet with daily vitamins and the occasional round of creatine. When I benched 305 pounds, I immediately aimed for 350; when I put up 355 pounds, I had my sights set on 400. There was no cap to the lunacy. I justified all the exercise with the "body is a temple" argument, even though my body was turning into the Coliseum. It was psychological; I wanted to be physically perfect for women and intimidating to other men.

I played rugby in college, and soon after moving to Texas I joined the Dallas Harlequins RFC. The lengthy commitment involved practices twice per week and Saturday matches. Women never seemed very impressed with my well-established corporate job, but they would swoon for foreign accents and brawny rugby players from England, Australia, Ireland, and South Africa. I learned some Afrikaans myself so I could take part in the antics at the drink-ups. I started to care more about rugby than anything else in my life, and I began living for the weekends.

Like every guy, I was a sports junkie. If I wasn't managing four fantasy football teams, I had March Madness brackets or I was scouting draft picks for fantasy basketball and baseball. I devoted hours to ESPN.com and Sonsofsamhorn.com, and I devoured every article by Peter Gammons and The Sports Guy, Bill Simmons. In fact, I subscribed to *ESPN the Magazine, Maxim, GQ, Details, Men's Health*, and *Men's Fitness* just so that I had something to do while I was eating breakfast or dinner. My continuing education involved a curriculum of "The Top 10 Female Erogenous Zones" and "Rock-hard Abs in 10 minutes" and "8 Signs Your Girlfriend is Cheating on You" and "Getting Drunk without the Gut." Though my stacks of literature were categorically puerile, and my fascination with them more curiosity than genuine interest, they attractively summarized, even created to a degree, my ambitions and absorptions. I was a normal guy.

My colleagues invested their time in similar pursuits, though some were the domestic type, managing their schedule around favorite TV shows and eagerly acquiring the latest Xbox or Play-

Station console. They built DVD libraries loaded up with movies like *There's Something About Mary* and *Super Troopers* and *National Lampoon's Van Wilder*, which fronted as harmless fare but subconsciously indoctrinated us with innumerable sexual references. If pot is the gateway drug to cocaine and heroin and LSD, then lewd, R-rated humor was the gateway to the greatest addiction confronting all of us: pornography. Porn had evolved from the small demographic of twelve year olds and truck drivers to overtake college campuses, but its popularity in corporate America couldn't be understated. There was no shame in it.

We lived for holidays like Halloween, New Year's, and St. Paddy's Day, because they gave us an occasion to be wildly immature. We were egocentric, each the lead character in our own epic movie. Our revelry reached its zenith on my twenty-third birthday. After our customary foray into alcoholic la-la land, an oncoming vehicle nearly steamrolled a new hire who had passed out in the parking lot of our apartment complex. Naturally, I was unshaken by the episode; it became yet another amusing story for the water cooler. I resigned myself to the fact that life beyond college offered very little personal change.

Amazingly, money eventually became a problem, and not that I had too much—I didn't have enough. My expenses, including rent, car payment, insurance, student loans, food, utilities, and credit card premiums became a heavy burden, and when dating and various other forms of socializing were factored into the mix (at nearly $1000 per month), my monthly expenditures approached $3500. After adjusting for tax withholdings and 401K deposits, I barely broke even. It was rather ironic: my boredom at work required that I look elsewhere for satisfaction; my lifestyle outside of the office demanded that I earn more money. This paradox instigated a renewed hunger for wealth.

My company transferred me one year later to Silicon Valley in California to the largest sales office in the world, and by the time I was twenty-four my compensation, including sales bonuses, had ballooned to $135,000. If there is such a thing as the "fast track," I was on it and steadily moving upward. My responsibilities began to increase significantly, and like a bulleted resume list of personal achievement, my numbers in every category of sales growth flew through the roof—and in a down market, no less. My customers and co-workers became role players in the non-stop stream of professional entertainment, and the resulting impact on my performance became obvious to everyone. I was a man on everyone's radar, and in a very short period of time I'd accomplished the success for which I'd always felt predestined. By every appearance the realization of my dreams was in full motion. I had a surplus of money. I was a business success story. I had a nice car. I traveled. I dated beautiful women. And yet strangely and unmistakably, I was still totally unsatisfied.

I began to understand how it is that movie stars who have fame, good looks, money, and every luxury can quickly spiral into alcoholism, drug-abuse, marital problems, and troubles with the law. There is no saturation point for earthly pleasure. There is no point when all the material benefits of the world add up to a general state of happiness. It is the Great Misconception. As I began taking a greater interest in business, I purchased several books written by millionaires and billionaires containing strategies for achieving unmatched success. Yet perhaps the most revealing nugget of truth contained in these books was that these titans of business were still *working*. I couldn't help but wonder, what is the point? These men devoted volumes addressing how to achieve the means, but they never offered the punch line: what is the *end*? G.K. Chesterton once wrote "Every man who knocks on the door of a brothel is looking for God." I finally began to understand what he meant by that. In all my diversions I was searching for God too; I just never found Him.

Ironically, despite my priorities, I considered myself to be a faithful man. I still continued to attend Mass, and I prayed nearly every night. I dragged my faith behind me into every aspect of my life, but it became a heavy burden of conscience that I shunned like an annoying relative. When I made an effort to embrace it, it offered less immediate gratification than doing what came naturally to me. But one Sunday morning, a particular scripture reading would begin to affect my outlook. The priest read from Apocalypse 3:15-16: "I know thy works, that thou art neither cold, nor hot. I would thou wert cold, or hot. But because thou art lukewarm, and neither cold, nor hot, I will begin to vomit thee out of my mouth."

The words didn't threaten me, they simply presented a logical point of fact: Living out one's faith is either no way to live or it's the only way to live; it's either imprisonment, or the only path to freedom. It offers happiness, or it frustrates the pursuit. There is no half-love, half-religion, half-worship, half-belief, half-truth. There is no *kinda-sorta*. I realized that my health demanded a decision, and my inability to make one had left me disenchanted. I was both a religious hypocrite and an employee who was impossible to satisfy.

I spent nearly three years in this quarter-life limbo, and my addictions shifted from sociaholic to workaholic and then back, all in pursuit of *something*. I struggled to commit to what I thought to be true and worthy of my devotion because it demanded a heroic, countercultural worldview. The mystery and majesty of God was an intensely cerebral and almost unattainable reality, while stimuli of every disordered variety summoned enchantingly to any brute. The words of St. Augustine began echoing in my own prayers: "I tell you this, my God, and confess to you those efforts for which I was praised; for at that time I believed that living a good life consisted in winning the favor of those who commended me. I failed to recognize the whirlpool of disgraceful conduct into which I had been flung, out of your sight." Though I had escaped some of the moral deprivations that infected so many my age, my morality was like a hair shirt that had become a constant irritant. A concerted effort to reorder my life became a journey of salvation far removed from the beaten path of normal Christian re-birth. My gut check occurred, of all places, in garlic country.

gut check

GILROY, THE "GARLIC CAPITAL OF THE WORLD," is a quiet town thirty-four miles southeast of San Jose in northern California. It is nestled into a fertile valley with several distinct geographies, from hilly vegetable rows arranged far into the distance, to flat, manure soaked fields teaming with livestock, and looming, dark green highlands reminiscent of the British Isles. One Friday evening in early summer I made a road trip to visit friends in Los Angeles, and the six-hour drive from the nation's bustling, high-tech epicenter to L.A.'s glitzy Hollywood backdrop is one that led me through this rural paradise. The winding road plunged and twisted as the setting sun cast long shadows throughout this poor man's Garden of Eden. The beauty of the countryside clashed with the pulse of my beat-heavy rap compilation, and it seemed to demand that I respect its innocence by switching to something lighter. With the windows rolled down the smell of garlic was palpable and pure, a far cry from the stale city smog. Though my compass aimed for a sprawling metropolis, it was this timeless scene that triumphed over the moment, a scene that was rich with simplicity.

My mind drifted to a different time period, before television and computers and professional sports, and before cars and cell phones, when men tilled the earth for six days a week and rested on Sunday to give thanks to God. I imagined what my life would have become had I been born in the 1800s, without the noise and the bustle of modern life. I pictured myself as a hard-working landowner with a quaint cottage and simple lifestyle, with little kids in the front yard playing with chickens and a gentle wife preparing a hearty meal. I could hear myself saying, "Yes ma'am" and "I reckon" and tipping my cap to the ladies and saying grace before meals. The man who guarded the front porch of the homestead was a man of great character and conviction, the man who I believed would have been me. But my cell phone interrupted the daydream.

"Wud up, brothah! You ready?" my buddy Tony shouted. He was a Lieutenant in the Navy stationed in San Diego, and he was driving up for the weekend.

"Yeah, kid. Definitely. It's been too long," I replied. I hadn't seen him in over a year.

"There are a couple places going off tonight, and I think I'll be able to get us into one place without paying cover. TJ is meeting up with us late night."

"Is he in town?" I asked.

"He said he wouldn't miss it."

"We got a crew! I'll see you soon, man. I'm about four, five hours away. I should get in around nine or ten."

"Hurry up. I'll have a drink waiting for you," he answered.

As I drove along the Five towards Bakersfield excited about the night, the word *lukewarm* remained in the front of my mind, and as much as I wanted to let the anticipation build for the evening's festivities, I couldn't shake the thought that I was hurting myself. Only with a certain sense of humility can a man see himself as he truly is, without taking comfort in the false notions of the person he thinks he is. I had learned long before that manhood isn't defined by age or rank or title, and it's not a measure of one's wealth or assets; manhood is shaped by character. The word *character* is often used loosely to describe athletes or politicians, or otherwise ignoble individuals, so implying that I lacked character seemed pretty harsh. I generally treated people with courtesy, I donated money to the Salvation Army Santa, I attended church, I hated communism, I supported our troops—I even wore a Livestrong bracelet. By everyday standards I was a fairly upstanding man.

But the nineteenth-century image of me was a different man entirely. He wasn't a gym rat, he wasn't lustful, and he didn't spend his weekends at the bar. Our priorities were very much opposite, though I wasn't sure if it was a product of the time period or our general beliefs. Maybe it was both. I was ruled by entertainment and the pleasures of being twenty-something and irresponsible; his world rotated on conviction. And then it hit me. It was like one of those rare epiphanies that causes black to become white, right to become left, down to become up, and so on, but it was very anticlimactic, anti-Hollywood. My car didn't swerve off the road; I didn't lose a loved one; and I didn't learn that I had cancer. I just came to a simple, obvious realization: the difference between that man and me was that *he thought about dying.* He must have.

This revelation was by no means profound, but the implications of it were. It led me to understand the cause of my discontent. All along I had been struggling with outcomes. *What was the goal? What was I working towards?* I hadn't placed much thought into the fact that the most certain, universal end goal is *death*. Our mortality binds all of us together, and in dying everyone's end becomes the same regardless of how we get there, like the finish line to a marathon. I had spent a large portion of my education, from biology to theology to philosophy, concerned with the origins of man, though the question with the greater ramifications is: *Where are we going?* What happens when we die? It would seem the general population can be divided into three categories: those who believe in some form of judgment at the hands of a Creator, those who don't believe in an afterlife, and those who just don't care either way. But for those in the first camp, the question becomes: *how* will we be judged?

At the end of every quarter and every year, my manager would arrange a meeting to set my quarterly objectives, and it would be his objectives that determined my daily activity. In business, if a meeting or a relationship or a customer call didn't help me to achieve my quarterly goals, I simply didn't waste my time. I possessed a disciplined focus, and it was a major reason for my success. My personal life was a different story.

My phone rang again. It was another buddy named Corey Rogers (a.k.a. C-Rog) who I knew from our office in L.A., and he knew all of my friends from our time together in Dallas. I debated whether or not I wanted to answer.

"C-Rog!" I announced, somewhat half-heartedly.

"T-money!! Are you driving Miss Daisy? What the hell is taking you so long??"

"Kid, I'm dodging staties left and right," I fired back. "They're pullin' over grandmothers right now."

"I'm already over at the pad and your beer is getting warm. Hurry your ass up!" he commanded.

"Put it on ice. I'm coming," I replied. By the end of the phone call I felt jolted by the age-old dilemma presenting itself once again. I badly wanted to party it up with my friends, but I so badly wanted to be a different guy.

There are those moments in everyone's life when you experience a feeling of disconnection to the world. Sometimes it creeps up suddenly, like after a death-defying three-hour power nap, when you wake up in a catatonic and disoriented haze. Then there are other times when a person's long-standing comprehension of the world is shattered by a profound wake-up call. Several buddies of mine, rowdy buddies, stopped partying for two weeks after they saw *The Passion of the Christ*. The movie rendered them speechless and so insecure that they couldn't even bear to watch *SportsCenter* highlights. Others enter an ethereal place when under extreme duress, like during the twenty-third mile of a marathon, or while caught in a catastrophe like an earthquake or a typhoon. It's no surprise that, immediately following 9-11, every church around the country was packed with people who seemed innately compelled to go despite their tepid belief in a higher power. There is a piece of us in quiet denial of our own insignificance and mortality, but when an event rattles the soul, be it emotionally or spiritually or otherwise, it becomes like smelling salt for our disillusionment.

During my sophomore year in college, I participated in a program called Spring Break Alternative, which sent twenty students to the far northern reaches of Maine near the Canadian border. We spent a long, exhausting week in the poorest area of a tiny town building homes for the underprivileged, but our work as Good Samaritans, though significant, made far less impact on the town than it did on our own social and spiritual outlook. Through the seclusion, the sour taste of poverty, and the camaraderie, we had been transported into an entirely alternate environment divorced from our habitual routine. Despite our brief time away, the experience left a powerful imprint, and the purity and simpleness of our venture made our return to normalcy a jarring transition. Not surprisingly, the awakening was not permanent as we quickly became reacquainted with our old habits, but the process of assimilating back into the college culture was nonetheless painful. Friends who have spent years abroad in Africa and South America through mission trips or Jesuit Volunteer Corps have reported similar strains upon returning home, but they had the benefit of total immersion and were better equipped for long-term change. I felt that familiar feeling returning again, but this time it wasn't the result of a physical estrangement.

By the time I had arrived in L.A., the boys were wound up and primed for the Sunset Strip. Our wardrobes had upgraded a bit since college—striped, spread collar, hundred dollar Hugo Boss dress shirts, Diesel jeans, and a variety of accoutrements from belt buckles to bracelets. Our burly friend, Phil, offset the monotony with a "Don't Hate Me Because I'm Beautiful" t-shirt. We ventured out to the club shortly before 11:00 PM, and ended up at a swank hotspot with a line of beautiful singles that swung around the block to the parking lot. We had two glaring strikes against us—there were no women in our party of roughly ten dudes, and we were underdressed—so if it weren't for the fact that a friend of Tony's played for the Angels, we would have had no chance at getting past the bouncers. Instead, we skipped the line and the cover, were given VIP access, and were greeted to friendly handshakes from the owner with the half-hug that only guys do.

"This place is off the hook!" said Phil, brimming with excitement.

"Who do we know again?" I asked.

"Tony's buddy from the Angels. They played ball at Arizona."

"Is he any good?"

"No, he sucks. His ERA is like 6 or something, but he's making like a mil per," he explained, more focused on the women decorating the VIP lounge than he was on my question.

The music was unbearably loud (a mixture of hip-hop and techno) and talking turned into shouting as we commented on the surroundings, the music, and the abundance of skin. Within thirty minutes the number of people had doubled, and before long each of us had our eyes locked on our favorite female. Two hundred dollar bottles of Belvedere dressed our table, and drinks were being mixed, passed, and thrown back like Gatorade at the Boston Marathon. The process repeated itself, and without the need to stand in line at the bar, we were drinking faster than normal. It was good catching up with my friends, and we joked about work and women, women and work, and we reminisced about our college days and how stupid we all were as twenty-year-olds. But despite how perfect the night was shaping up to be, I had an impossible time livening up, and it became noticeable.

"T, what's wrong with you, kid? Loosen up. You seem stiff," commanded Tony about an hour into the celebration. Before I could respond TJ emerged between the VIP stanchions to thunderous shouts and bear hugs, and two drinks were shoved into his palms to catch up.

"AHHHHH!"

"TJ!!!!!!!!!! What up brothah!!" the boys shouted.

The music continued to pump through the sound system, seemingly louder than ever. It felt like our own soundtrack. The dance floor started to pick up, and one incredibly jacked bodybuilder with a shaved chest had already removed his shirt before one of the bouncers forced him to put it back on. The showdown almost came to violence before a mediator stepped in to cool everyone off. One handshake–half-hug later all was right again with the world.

"T-money!" shouted C-Rog into my ear, while also spraying half of my cheek with his saliva. "That group of girls over at the bar has been giving us the eye for, like, half an hour. Go bring them up here."

"Why me? You do it. Grow some chest hair."

"C'mon, man. You're the sales guy! You're good at this s—."

"T-Saab, go do it!" added Phil.

I shook my head and finished my drink. I stepped down to the main floor and over to the bar where a group of five thinly dressed girls were huddled together, each sipping their own multi-colored drink. They turned their back to me as I approached.

"Hey!" I announced, getting their attention. "My boys want to know if you want to hang out with us."

"Who are your boys?" said the least attractive of the five.

"The ones you've been staring at for the last twenty minutes," I smiled.

"You're cocky!" shouted girl number two.

"I'm honest. Don't shoot the messenger."

After a few shoulder shrugs, half smiles, and head tilts within their closed circle, the girls arrived at a consensus and followed me back to the lion's den, where the posturing began in earnest.

"You are the man, T-Saab," mumbled C-Rog, with a discrete handshake as I made it up the steps. "How do you always do that?!"

"I told them you were the leading man in *Titanic 2*. Go get'em, player."

The best-looking girl in the clique was a tan, 5'5" brunette with blue eyes and thick, curly hair that dangled midway down her back. She was toned and groomed and athletic like all the other Cali girls on the Strip, and she walked elegantly. I assumed that she was Italian or Spanish.

"I'm Whitney, by the way!" she shouted, cutting through the slight awkwardness after we had made eye contact. So many of us had squeezed into the VIP area that we were now pressed up against each other.

"Tarek!" I shouted in her ear.

"What is it?!" she frowned, either confused by the name or already deaf from the music.

"Uh, Derek," I said, in order to avoid the whole back-story. It was close enough.

"Nice to meet you!" she smiled.

"Likewise!" I nodded.

"How come it took you so long to talk to us?" she asked, fishing for something to say.

"I didn't want to talk to you," I replied truthfully, taking no care to censor my words. In different circumstances meeting her would have been the pinnacle of my night, but between the noise and the environment, I was cynical about meeting anyone of substance, and I just wasn't in the mood.

"You're a jerk!" she declared while recoiling, but before she could turn away, I grabbed her elbow.

"You're right. You're right. I didn't mean it that way at all. I'm a jerk," I confessed, not meaning to hurt her feelings. "I just meant to say I haven't been in the mood to talk tonight, but I do want to talk to you."

In reality, few people were talking. The DJ made certain of that, but I put forth the effort nonetheless.

"What are you girls doing tonight? Special occasion?" I asked.

"Yeah, we're celebrating FREEDOM!" she announced, looking back towards her friends.

"Like, in a George Bush kinda way? Must be expensive," I joked, but she didn't get it and furrowed her brow.

"What?! No, I just broke up with my boyfriend. So did my friend Samantha. It's girl's night out!" she replied, before sucking on her straw and casting a long glance at me. She smelled like vanilla.

"How long were you dating?!" I shouted above the music.

"Six years!" My eardrums could feel what she was saying, but I could barely hear it.

"Wow! Really? How old are you?" I said, taken back.

"Twenty-three!"

"Did you love him?" I asked.

"What?!" she laughed, caught off guard by my question. "What kind of question is that? Of course I loved him! I lived with the guy. But it was just time, ya know? F— it. Carpe diem!"

I nodded my head and made a face as if to say "sure," but I was certain there was more emotional baggage attached to her comment than she let on. A breakup like hers was basically a divorce, and even if I had the opportunity to date her, beauty and all, I would've passed based on that knowledge alone. And her language wasn't very attractive either.

"Well, congrats, I guess!" I replied.

"Thank you!" she answered, and as she said it, 50 Cent's "In Da Club" launched an exuberant reaction from the crowd:

"YEEEEEEAAAHHHHHHH!!!!" screeched the girls, arms raised in the air.

"GO SHAWTY! IT'S YO BIRTHDAY! GON' PARTY LIKE IT'S YO BIRTHDAY!! WE GON' SIP BACARDI LIKE IT'S YOUR BIRTHDAY!!!!" everyone howled in unison.

"C'mon. Let's dance!!" shouted Whitney, grabbing my hand and dragging me to the main level. The dance floor quickly jammed with people, and the girls sang, wriggled, and gyrated amongst each other, lapping up the attention while the guys packed together to watch. This feel good period in the night was overflowing with high fives, arms around necks, and dozens of *Good to see you*s.

Though my head bobbed to the beat, I stood otherwise motionless and unaffected, meditating on what it all added up to. Trapped inside that large, pulsating swarm in the steamy, sweaty basement, I felt much closer to hell than I did to heaven. And this was a good night. I didn't want to be the one guy in the group bringing down the vibe, but I couldn't shake the fear of an earthquake wiping us all out in that instant, and what I'd have to show for my final waking moments. I didn't fear death; I feared that I was failing my life.

"YOU BETTER LOSE YOURSELF IN THE MUSIC! THE MOMENT! YOU OWN IT! YOU BETTER NEVER LET IT GO! YOU ONLY GET ONE SHOT!" chanted the crowd in harmony with Eminem's hit single.

Even as Jay-Z, Outkast, Nellie, and others brought the throng to a suspended frenzy, I reflected on faith and truth with a fist-ful of Belvedere, sip after numbing sip. The discord between my environment and my mindset was as pronounced as ever. My understanding of the universe, and man's place in it, had been well formed in years past: Aquinas and Augustine; Anselm and Thomas More; Chrysostom and Athanasius; I had studied them all in college, and I embraced them. They shaped my worldview. I concluded, and reaffirmed with time, that either the Catholic faith was the one, true faith, or there was no God at all. Nothing else made any sense. But despite my best intentions, I was *still* unable to summon the strength to act in accordance with my beliefs in all phases of my life. I *still* compartmentalized my devotion. As in college, the influence of my surroundings played an integral role in my devolution, and in direct conflict with my conscience, I was *still* a co-conspirator in the reckless behavior with my friends.

In that moment of isolation, against the cadence of a hip-hop beat, I recalled Aristotle's lesson from years before, that "the success of man's ability to live the excellent, virtuous life determines his happiness." But our common human journey toward death —that single, equalizing moment—is a journey devoid of purpose without an outcome for our activity, without a judgment for how we've lived. If happiness is the only outcome, than the finality of our lives actually impairs that happiness. A happiness that ends is the worst type of tragedy. It is partially this reason that Aristotle says true happiness can never be achieved on earth, but only in the afterlife.

As flickering red stage lights interrupted the darkness, I retreated into myself, a tortoise into his shell. Recreation was an important part of healthy living, I acknowledged, but this was counterproductive. I was regressing. I had duped myself into believing that I could maintain an honorable life while still attached to my worldly interests, but I was becoming aware that those interests had the power to dissociate me from honorable living. Aristotle lived over three hundred years before Christ, but I venture to say that if he had known Christ he would have adjusted his statement to: "the success of man's ability to live the excellent, virtuous life determines his happiness, *and that begins with Christ who is the model of all virtues.*"

"GIRL I'M FEELIN' WHAT YOU FEELIN'! NO MORE HO-PIN' AND WISHIN'! I'M ABOUT TO TAKE MY KEY AND

STICK IT IN THE IGNITION!!" echoed R. Kelly throughout the dark lounge.

"So gimme that TOOT TOOT!! Lemme give you that BEEP BEEP!!" bellowed my friend Ben along to the tune, before turning towards me. "T, you alright? You haven't been yourself tonight. What gives?"

"Yeah, man. Livin' the dream," I replied, unconvincingly.

"I don't buy it."

"I think I'm just getting tired of this scene, man."

"This has been an awesome night, kid!" he said. "What's your problem?!"

Ben and I had been friends since my senior year in college. He'd flown in from Kansas City where he worked in finance, and he understood me better than any of the other guys. He came from a large Catholic household of eight children, and he wasn't just nominally Catholic. His faith was important to him.

"It's great seeing you, don't get me wrong. It's awesome, kid. I always love hanging out with you!" I said, trying to express my genuine sentiment. "This scene is just depressing. It's like a giant orgy. I feel like I should be helping people or something, ya know?"

"You can do more good here than anywhere, T. These are the people who need it the most, brother. St. Francis said, 'preach the gospel, and when necessary use words.'"

"We're not preaching here, man," I stated matter-of-factly.

"Jesus went to the prostitutes and the tax collectors," he countered.

"Yeah, but He wasn't getting hammered with'em," I argued. "What type of gospel are we preaching?"

"We're not having sex and getting drunk. We're showing you can live out your faith in the real world and still be normal have a good time."

"We're eight drinks deep and we're slobbering on girls. What's the distinction? How does that make us any different?" I asked.

He stared at me blankly.

"This is getting old for me, man."

—

AFTER RETURNING HOME from my L.A. excursion, I dug out the list of the man I wished to be, which had been buried deep in a box of assorted memorabilia. I reexamined it for quite some time, aware of its validity but decidedly gun shy. I also uncovered a quote from St. Augustine that seemed particularly relevant: "Such a creature's good is to hold fast to You always, lest by turning away it lose the light it acquired by its conversion, and slip back into the old life, dark and abysmal." I meditated upon my list with great earnestness, recognizing ever more clearly how these intellectual and spiritual desires conflicted with the man I really was. Striving to become the perfect gentlemen would come with excessive limitations, I worried, and in some ways, I felt like it was a necessity to be thuggish in order to retain a sense of my own masculinity. No one wants to be Ned Flanders. Yet despite my fear of becoming "soft," my growing distaste for my habits offered enough motivation to ignore the social pressures and forge ahead. The battleground for my interior struggle was emerging, a battle of the *ordinary*.

As I rummaged through the few keepsakes that remained of my uninspiring past, I found a very small collection of books that had survived from my college years. Since I had traded in most of my textbooks for cash at the end of each semester, I only had a few inexpensive paperbacks left. One of them, *The Screwtape Letters* by C.S. Lewis, I had never actually read, but I noticed it and thumbed through its pages searching for wisdom or any quotable passage I could use for inspiration. The book captivated me because of its bluntness and its accuracy, and I inhaled every word as one devil educates another on humans, our flaws, and how to exploit them. In chapter after chapter I recognized similarities with my deplorable behavior, but I continued reading on like a masochist looking for answers. One passage in particular so closely described me that I thought to myself: I *am* that guy!

He can be induced to live, as I have known many humans live, for quite long periods, two parallel lives; he will not only appear to be, but actually be, a different man in each of the circles he frequents. Failing this, there is a subtler and more entertaining method. He can be made to take a positive pleasure in the perception that the two sides of his life are inconsistent. This is done by exploiting his vanity. He can be taught to enjoy kneeling beside the grocer on Sunday just because he remembers that the grocer could not possibly understand the urbane and mocking world which he inhabited on Saturday evening; and contrariwise, to enjoy the bawdy and blasphemy over the coffee with these admirable friends all the more because he is aware of a "deeper," "spiritual" world within him which they cannot understand. You see the idea—the worldly friends touch him on one side and the grocer on the other, and he is the complete, balanced, complex man who sees round them all. Thus, while being permanently treacherous to at least two sets of people, he will feel, instead of shame, a continual undercurrent of self-satisfaction. Finally, if all else fails, you can persuade him, in defiance of conscience, to continue the new acquaintance on the ground that he is, in some unspecified way, doing these people "good" by the mere fact of drinking their cocktails and laughing at their jokes, and that to cease to do so would be "priggish," "intolerant," and (of course) "Puritanical."

It was vital that I make a clean break from my routine, but without the benefit of physical isolation, I was forced to create a sense of separation the hard way. For a few weeks, I chose to quit drinking and frequenting the bars, and I cut out all vulgar music and threw away every mindless magazine. I also made every effort to clean up my foul language and to pray more. But the purification process, despite my best intentions, became a grinding and vigorous battle with my own sullied predilections. It hurt. In Matthew 11:12, Jesus proclaims, "From the days of John the Baptist until now, the kingdom of heaven suffereth violence, and the violent bear it away." The violence He is speaking of is obviously not an armed resistance against an external enemy; it is an interior violence against our own perversity. At every temptation I wanted to quit and submit to the whim of the moment, but death became a target for me, a flashing lighthouse that urged caution and perseverance.

Several weeks later, after confessing my struggles to a priest, he recommended a book entitled *The Spiritual Combat* by an Italian named Dom Lorenzo Scupoli. It was neat and compact, and its strong language addressed my modern-day conflict with precision even though it was written in the sixteenth century. I read its passages and discovered what I knew to be true but couldn't really articulate:

> We shall see clearly that what the world pursues with such eagerness and perfection is mere vanity and illusion; that ambition and pleasure are dreams which, once shattered, are succeeded by sorrow and regret; that ignominy is a subject of glory, and sufferings a source of joy; that nothing can be

more noble or approach the divine nature more closely than
to forgive those who injure us, and to return good for evil.

We shall see clearly that it is greater to despise the world
than to have it at one's command; that it is infinitely prefer-
able to submit to the humblest of men for God's sake, than
to command kings and princes; that an humble knowledge
of ourselves surpasses the deepest sciences; in short, that
greater praise is due to him who curbs his passions on the
most trivial occasions, than to him who conquers the stron-
gest cities (and) defeats entire armies.

Any guy like me can act like the masses, I thought, but maintaining virtue in the face of great opposition demands a for-
midable resoluteness. As Chesterton says, "A dead thing can go
with the stream, but only a living thing can go against it." For
a period of time I figured it was possible to do just about anything, but my weaknesses made it difficult for me to maintain
initiatives for very long. I wanted to be virtuous, but not always
at the moment. As St. Augustine once famously said "Lord give
me chastity, just not yet." I could have made a similar statement
about any of my vices.

But the more steadily I battled, and the longer I operated
under the premise that I would never find happiness in pleasure,
material possessions, women, fame, power, or any other worldly
luxury, the more passionate I became in my desire for *heaven*.
This craving began to permeate my behavior. With heaven as
the ultimate goal in my march toward death, I wondered: what
is the *least* amount of work that it takes to get there? I reflected
on what my life had become, on who I was, and on the man I
wanted to be. I had removed the foggy lenses of impropriety to
view a spectacle of great satisfaction, and the only questioned
that remained was: *now what?*

eight

eye of a needle

B Y THE TIME I HAD FINISHED my second year in the San Jose sales office and my third full year in corporate America, my perspective on life had changed so significantly that my job and my relationships began to change as well. The transformation was slow, but I started looking past my next promotion, past my next bonus, past the next "attaboy" and gold star, and rediscovered the true function of labor: to support my future family and myself, and to help me get to heaven.

I noticed that many of my friends, like me, had become wrapped up in the normal obsessions of wealth, women, and entertainment in its various forms. But there were others who avoided the capitalist mania entirely, to the point of unemployment or total apathy. By age twenty-five, a large number of my peers hadn't left home, and some hadn't finished college, opting instead for high school jobs while living in perpetual teenager land. Coddled by family and society, they had no reason to develop a career at all. Their common excuses were "I don't know what I really want to do with my life" and "I want to stay young forever." Society affords many people that option, and without the pressure of survival, there is little necessity to take on responsibility. My generation of twenty-somethings has given birth to the phrase "quarter-life crisis" because of the anxiety that comes with the knowledge that living the next fifty years of your life as Joe Normal before you die is a less-than-glamorous proposition.

Not long ago, *Esquire* (July 2006) polled fifty-one twenty-five year-old American men and asked them about manhood. Their responses offer an excellent representation of the mainstream:

> "I'm not really ready to make sacrifices for anyone other than myself. I realize that's selfish, but I'm not really sure what to do about it."—*JW, Alabama, engineer*

> "I'd like to find a new job. Something that offers me a sense of purpose. I feel like Peter Gibbons prehypnosis, and no one should have to feel like that."—*KB, Arkansas, bank teller*

> "I entered manhood, realized it sucked, and am working on reverting back to childhood. A lot of people I know have the rock-star/movie-star dream, and we dread the clock ticking on middle-agedness."—*JJ, Kentucky, robotics specialist*

> "I often think I should be a bit more reckless and carefree. After all, I'm only twenty-five. A lot of my friends don't even know what to do with their lives yet. Society tells us that's irresponsible, but I actually think it can be the smarter, more mature thing to do."—*EM, Indiana, graphic designer*

> "If manhood means you have to grow and stop having fun and act like a boring adult, then no, I haven't reached manhood. I don't know if I ever will."—*JE, New Jersey, deejay and event promoter*

"I couldn't wait to be twenty-one, but after that birthday there are no more privileges. I remember turning twenty-two and realizing that I didn't want to get older. I still feel that way, but I won't lose sleep over it until I'm twenty-nine."—*KF, New Hampshire, skier*

"I still like all the things I liked when I was a kid – breakfast cereal, *Quantum Leap* reruns, action figures. I don't feel like I could raise a child, care for a wife, or do manual labor. This is what made you a man in 1950. Lord knows what makes you one now."—*ST, New York, TV editing assistant*

"Being twenty-five allows you in one instance to be crazy and party, and then, the very next day, close a real estate deal or buy stock." —*TB, So. Carolina, Merchant Marine*

I had finally reached a point in my life where I recognized my problem, but living out the solution became my biggest obstacle. Since devotion to God is an all-encompassing affair, acting in accordance with my beliefs demanded a broad and absolute commitment. Work was no exception. Career ambitions or personal dreams, though admirable in their own right, become fundamentally disordered (and a waste of time) if they cause us to lose sight of our eternal objective. "For what doth it profit a man, if he gain the whole world, and suffer the loss of his own soul? Or what exchange shall a man give for his soul?" Undoubtedly, one human being is more valuable than all of the world's riches, so to barter my soul for material gain or carnal pleasures was to make a gigantic, Faustian blunder.

All my life I had been groomed to be as successful as possible, and my life was governed by the notion that my level of wealth and responsibility established my self-worth. Anything less than over-achievement would have been a letdown. My job was more of a competitive sport than it was a profession, and I wanted to be seen as a champion of business. Many of my co-workers struggled through failed marriages due to the stress their careers placed on the family, but they persisted because the corporate hierarchy was powerful, both inside and outside the company, and the power offered honor and validation. At the time I wasn't married, so I was free to enslave myself to the pursuit of promotions, raises, and bonuses, and I often toiled ninety hours per week, including full days on Sunday. The Third Commandment was for slackers, I convinced myself, not for talented businessmen. Ironically, I had chosen an engineering major in college so that I could work less than my blue-collar father, yet I found myself working longer despite my inflated income. Nowhere in this picture was my belief in God a factor.

But I began to realize that all of it added up to nothing more than fuel for my vanity, so I started speaking to people with greater courtesy and professionalism, and buffed my e-mails with a more cordial polish. I diverted praise to those in the office who were less often recognized for their contributions. My interest in awards evaporated, and I instead took more interest in helping team members make it through the challenges of the day. I merged my career goals with the greatest goal—making it to heaven—and I adjusted my actions accordingly. Even though I worked less (and stopped working on Sundays altogether), I lost little in the way of productivity because I was more committed. When I embraced my beliefs, I became more ethical, more truthful, more helpful, more courteous, more likeable, more responsible, and altogether more rational. I was a better businessman because of the change. The sum gain was the reward I really sought all along—a sense of purpose.

"Saab, you going to lunch?" asked my officemate Justin, roughly four months after my trip to Los Angeles. Justin was thirty years old and well respected by everyone in the office. He was a Stanford grad and managed nearly fifteen million dollars in sales revenue through three sales accounts.

"You up for Sushi?" I asked in reply.

"You eat more Sushi than anyone I've met in my life," he responded, shaking his head with a smirk. "Don't you get sick of it?"

"If you're gonna be a bear, be a grizzly!" I cracked.

"You better watch your mercury levels, man. I'm serious," he advised, like a concerned parent.

"I'm not pregnant," I responded candidly. "The day I can tell you the temperature without a thermostat I'll back off a bit, alright?"

The sushi bar was a short distance from the office, and we arrived early before the big lunch rush. The wait staff and the sushi chefs all knew us, and they greeted us immediately as we entered the doorway. A young waitress smiled and pointed us to our seat, clearly reluctant to unveil her English.

"What's been goin' on? How's business?" he asked, as he flipped through the menu. "What are you getting?"

"I always go for number four. You get twelve pieces and a bowl of Miso for twelve bucks. It's the lunch special," I explained. "Things are going well. Can't complain. You?"

"I'm alright. I'm getting a little stressed about account reviews, but besides that I'm okay."

The waitress came over and took our order, and we continued our conversation over a pot of green tea, briefly commenting on how much more attentive Asian waitresses are over their American counterparts.

"How do you think you'll do in reviews?" he asked, before burning his mouth.

"I'll get the same feedback I get every time. *Good job but you need to do better.* No one ever gets a standing ovation," I replied.

"Depressing, isn't it?"

"Yeah, somewhat," I chuckled. "But I think they're mostly concerned with the effort. Results they can coach, but they can't coach effort. I'm not too worried about it."

"They stress me out," he said, looking towards a large party of businessmen filing through the entrance. "There are a lot of question marks this quarter with my two biggest accounts."

"What are your plans for the future? Do you see yourself staying here forever?" I asked, leaning back as the waitress placed a steaming bowl of soup on my placemat.

"Your food will come out soon!" she said as she bowed.

"Thanks!" we replied in unison.

"I think I'm going to go back to business school," Justin continued. "I want to work for a venture capital firm."

"Why is that?"

"I've just always been interested in emerging markets, and with my technical background, I think I'd have a lot to offer, particularly in the Bay," he explained. "And working for a vc is where the real money is."

"Then what?"

"Probably something involving finance. I'd like to be a cfo somewhere," he said. "I also have some pretty strong ideas about where the future of technology is headed, things that I don't think a lot of people see. I may try to take advantage of that and get in at the ground floor of the market. The contacts you make in business school are more valuable than the education, ya know? I can see myself hooking up with a couple of guys and maybe putting something together."

Justin was that rare type of person with the raw intelligence to ace the sats, but a social demeanor that was neither abrasive nor eccentric. He had that ivy-league look and formality about him.

He was tall, with neatly combed hair and wire-framed glasses, and could have easily been mistaken for a pediatrician or high school English teacher, but not a fireman.

"Are you going to go back to Stanford?"

"Maybe. We'll see where I get in. Wharton would probably be my first choice, but I'll apply to Harvard and INSEAD and London Business School," he said, with the confidence of knowing he would get into one, if not all. "There's no point going to business school unless you get into one of the top schools. Like I said, it's all about the contacts. You're not going to meet the next great wave of entrepreneurs going to night school."

"I'll be honest, I never had you pegged as the entrepreneurial type. I always figured you for a lifer moving up the chain of command," I replied. Justin and I were acquaintances more than friends, and our brief interactions were typically non-intrusive.

"Business is my passion, man. It's in my blood. I breathe it. I've learned a lot here, but its time for me to expand my horizons, capture my full potential," he said. "What about you? How long do you plan on staying with the company?"

"To be honest, once I get my student loans paid off, I may just move somewhere quiet and be a teacher or something. I don't know," I answered, knowing as I said it that my response would elicit a surprised reaction.

"A teacher, eh?" he smiled, with a face that said *You've got to be joking*. "Get ready to make some sacrifices. Teachers don't make *anything*."

"I know, but I don't think I need very much."

"I just can't see it. You, of all people!" he laughed. "You have no patience for that. Who are you kidding? All it would take is one punk mouthing off at you before you tell him you're gonna knock his teeth in. They'd kick you out of there in a week!"

We then continued to have a good laugh about other would-be scenarios, like how I'd treat a child with a bladder issue or one with a weak excuse for missing homework.

"Yeah, well, I'll believe it when I see it," he replied after a brief pause, raising his eyebrows. "And like I said, those paychecks will get old quick." His skepticism was justifiable. Becoming a high school math teacher, as important and dignified as that role is, simply doesn't carry the same esteem as a corporate director with one hundred and fifty underlings. I remember growing up hearing the expression that "knowledge is power," but experience had taught me that, in reality, money is power. During my first year on the job my friends and I would joke: "Clothes don't make the man; *money* makes the man." The freedom to travel and buy what I wanted, when I wanted, possessed a narcotic attraction. The more I had, the more I needed, and perhaps more importantly, I loved the respect that came with affluence.

"Ya know, you're probably right Justin. The grass is always greener," I acknowledged. "I haven't put much thought into it."

"You're good at what you do now, man."

"Ya know what it is more than anything?" I asked rhetorically. "I don't feel free. I feel constricted."

"At work?

"Yeah."

"Take a vacation," he said, animatedly.

"From what? It's not like the work ever goes away. It'll just pile up and wait for me, and then I'll have to work overtime to catch up," I replied. "I mean real freedom. I want to be able to live my life before I'm sixty, man. See the world."

"If that's the case, you need ten million dollars and a good financial planner. You don't want to be a teacher."

"Yeah," I laughed. "I need to win the lottery."

We finished our lunch and squared up the tab.

"I'll tell you what, man. When you're teaching third graders you can forget about sushi lunches," he said, mocking me. "Eat up now while you have the cash."

My spending habits did present a problem. In the following weeks, I thought more about the future of my career. In a company with thirty thousand employees, there were jobs less fast-paced and demanding than sales in Silicon Valley, but few of them paid as well. As a general rule, the closer one is to the sale, the more money he makes. Yet I often wondered what my prosperity meant in consideration of the scriptural teaching: "It is easier for a camel to pass through the eye of a needle, than for a rich man to enter into the kingdom of God." It appeared to me that if Christ's warning was to be taken seriously, it was universally damning for an entire segment of people without any judgment on merit. Furthermore, I wondered, what about the powerful kings and queens in Christendom who are to this day praised for their valor and their saintly disposition despite their material abundance? I wanted to be one of *them*—a wealthy saint.

Out of curiosity, I purchased a biography of St. Louis ix of France by Jean de Joinville. I was hoping I would discover some enlightenment on Christ's admonition of the wealthy. St. Louis inherited the throne of France and all of its riches, and yet somehow he circumvented "the needle." But through reading his biography, I was left with a clearer understanding of Jesus's message. What I discovered was a profoundly righteous and irreproachable example of Christ-like behavior:

Right from the time of his childhood King Louis had compassion on the poor and suffering. It was his custom, wherever he went, to entertain a hundred and twenty poor persons every day in his own house, and feed them with bread and wine, meat or fish. In Lent and Advent the number of poor was increased; and it often happened that the king served them himself; setting their food before them, carving their meat, and giving them money with his own hand as they left. . . .

Besides all this, he bade a number of old and crippled men to dine or sup with him every day near his own table, and ordered them to be served with the same food as himself; after they had eaten they were each given a certain sum of money to take away.

In addition to this, every day the king used to give generous alms to poor monks and nuns, to ill-endowed hospitals, to poor sick persons, and to religious communities with little money. He was equally generous in his gifts to men and women of gentle birth in need, to homes for fallen women, to poor widows and to women in labor, as also to poor craftsmen who through age or sickness could no longer ply their trade. His benefactions were indeed so numerous that they could hardly be reckoned.

The Life of St. Louis opened my eyes to the fallacy of the Joel Osteen "prosperity gospel" mindset. Having wealth is a great blessing, but it is a great burden also, because *attachment* to wealth thoroughly separates us from God. In J.R.R. Tolkein's trilogy *The Lord of the Rings*, Frodo Baggins holds the most powerful and valuable ring in the entire world, a prize so tempting that nearly everyone desires it, even though it has destroyed every creature who ever possessed it. The pursuit of the ring and its tremendous power provoke behavior so despicable and barbaric that it is no coincidence the humblest creature, a hobbit, is picked to destroy it. The parallel to man's present-day infatuation with wealth is uncanny, because just as in the case of the ring, our attraction to wealth can be so overwhelming that it saps the life-blood out of our souls.

I began to realize that the power we seek in the form of wealth and title and material possessions isn't power in its purest form. Power isn't having the world at your fingertips; it is having the world at your fingertips and being able to give it up! Virtually anyone, especially in our culture, can be wealthy or famous or powerful; in fact, most people in America today have more luxuries than Solomon in all his glory. But very few seem capable of maintaining their prosperity while still developing their virtue and spirituality. It is only with the mastery of our inclinations, I assumed, that we begin to experience true freedom and open ourselves up to the Divine. It is a power built upon the rock of humility and self-control. The tail end of Jesus' Sermon on the Mount explains this with great clarity: "Lay not up to yourselves treasures on earth: where the rust, and moth consume, and where thieves break through and steal. But lay up to yourselves treasures in heaven: where neither the rust nor moth doth consume, and where thieves do not break through, nor steal. For where thy treasure is, there is thy heart also . . . No man can serve two masters. For either he will hate the one, and love the other: or he will sustain the one, and despise the other. You cannot serve God and mammon."

The message of "detachment from the world" is as old as Christianity. The monks and priests and nuns throughout history who dedicated their lives to God seemed to comprehend and live out this reality, sacrificing all the pleasures of the world in pursuit of holiness. Though my vocation was different, the act of consecrating my life to God seemed no less necessary. The onslaught of my quarter-life crisis resulted from the pursuit of an illusion, an egocentric hunger that could never truly be satisfied. As I turned my attention to the ascetic life, I became less encumbered by title or wealth or vainglory. I determined that there was nothing that offered any real incentive to turn my thoughts from God and my final judgment. But it required training of the most difficult and countercultural sort. At least the monks and the nuns had each other. I felt totally alone.

part three

nine

detachment

L IKE MOST TWENTY-SOMETHINGS, I shared a place with
roommates, and our 1970s condo in Santa Clara was one
part home, one part college dormitory. It was nice enough
for a family, but worn enough to be abused without concern. It
was a bachelor pad. We bought a foosball table for the dining
room and a grill for the patio. There were posters on every wall
just like in college, only this time they were framed, which added
to the aura of adulthood. One of the guys contributed a 46-inch
television, and we had a DVD library loaded with the potty-humor
classics and the manly must-haves like *Rocky* and *Gladiator*, and
a music library jammed with everything from Jackson Browne
to Tupac. We had a PlayStation 2 with *NHL '03* and *Madden '04*.
The sink was perpetually stocked with dirty dishes despite the
fact that we usually grilled or ate out, so we hired a maid to keep
us as close to sanitary as possible. The condo exhibited most of
the stereotypes attributed to guys living the post-college life, and
fell somewhere in the mean between cockroaches and class—not
totally disgusting, but not exactly fit for mothers.

I had the middle-sized room upstairs, and it was as much a storage unit as it was a bedroom. With each passing night, the clutter I had been collecting since high school made me feel more claustrophobic. In life, there are necessities, there are luxuries, and then there's just junk. I decided that it was time for me to jettison all of my useless cargo, and it was a spiritual decision more than a practical one. I took a literalist approach to the term detachment, and felt that taking ownership of my spirituality came through a certain absence of material ownership. The less I allowed myself to have, the more I could focus on the matters of greatest importance.

I went through my closet and filled three garbage bags with clothes. If I didn't wear it, I didn't want it. I reduced my dress shirts from thirty to about fifteen, and in similar fashion went through my suits, jeans, and dress pants. I had an enormous collection of T-shirts—free T-shirts, prize T-shirts, work T-shirts, college T-shirts, gym T-shirts, goin' out T-shirts—but I wore only about ten in a steady rotation, so I dumped the rest, along with old socks and old ball caps. I gathered all of my extra sneakers, extra cleats, extra dress shoes; old ties from my private school years; doubles of pictures and extra office supplies; old posters and knick-knacks, giveaways and mementos.

I decided that I could manage with ten pens instead of eighty; one stapler instead of two; one baseball bat instead of four. I loaded my entire music collection onto my computer and sold the original CDs. I sold my collection of 5,000 baseball cards on eBay. I dumped my "miscellaneous" tub of old cables from a lifetime of electronics, because I couldn't remember the last time I had used any of them. I sold what I could, gave away what I couldn't, and trashed the rest. By the end of my frenzy, my room was barren and hotel-like, and a significant portion of my youth was discarded. I felt more like a traveler in my own home, which I realized I was.

St. Paul writes, "When I was a child, I spoke as a child, I understood as a child, I thought as a child. But, when I became a man, I put away the things of a child." He instructs Christians to make this break not only with belongings, but also in mentality. The phrase "I'm just a big kid" bears a very hazardous connotation. A child is attached. He is attached to a bottle, to his mother, to his needs, to amusements, and to his friends. To be a real man is to be unattached—not from responsibility or justice—rather, from those dependencies that inhibit responsibility and justice.

A man understands that he is designed for no other purpose than to be united to God, and this desire calls for self-denial, though maintaining an ascetic lifestyle in our modern playground is like asking an eight-year-old to study long division at an arcade. It runs contrary to the world's dictum that "happiness can be found on earth." It requires discipline and the acute awareness that God is present in every aspect of our existence. He is unavoidable. It was mystifying for me to think of God at the movie theatre; God at the gym; God at the condo; God at the office; God at the Taco Cabana and every dive restaurant or hangout.

My bedroom became a reflection of my spiritual transition, a process of cutting away the fat. My roommates observed the outward signs of cleanliness with amusement and laughter, but they politely respected the change in my spirituality with genuine interest. As I began to acknowledge God's omnipresence in my mind, my habits imitated my thoughts. Living the faith became a serious matter. For much of my adult life I approached my faith strictly through intellectual reasoning and curiosity, and anything left unanswered I reluctantly accepted on belief. But through my struggles I came to realize that God could not be studied abstractly and totally understood. To know God fully is to either love Him or reject Him. Intellect forms the conscience, but an intellectual epiphany will not heal a lifetime of addiction to error. The tipping point in my struggle came when I began to fully capitulate to my heart and will, in conjunction with education and belief. I simply could no longer maintain the friction of two opposing forces and call it "well-roundedness." I made a decision, and my love for God won out.

The act of separation from the bar scene and from my other vices left a gaping void in my life, both in time and in their lease on satisfaction. In the past, I let the void hang out in the open like a missing tooth until I felt compelled to replace it with another vice. But in my quest for detachment I found myself yearning to replace the voids through spiritual fulfillment. Unfortunately, I felt uninspired in the one place I was drawn to the most—church.

Catholic Churches are like a box of chocolates, to borrow the analogy from Forrest Gump, you never know what you're gonna get—especially in California. I attended Mass at my local parish like I had every Sunday, but I still failed to connect with the promise of mystery in my Catholic belief. Absorbing the mind-numbing strum of sappy, seductive guitar hymns, or the fiftieth iteration of the "God loves you" sermon from a happy-go-lucky preacher, was a gut-wrenching experience for any man with an ounce of testosterone. Flowery emotional appeals don't resonate well with pragmatic men, which is probably why men have an aversion to modern churches.

As I read every classic Christian work I could handle by the Doctors of the Church, I took greater notice at how the world I was battling to leave had found its way into the world I sought to embrace. In my local church, like many others, the treasured masterpieces of Catholic art were replaced in favor of sandal-clad caricatures with all the realism of a Hanna-Barbera cartoon. It could have been tolerable if I had sensed any level of reverence from the community, but apathy had found a new home in the cargo shorts and unkempt appearance of communicants, while others claimed to be "on fire" with a form of trendy, secular Christianity. Women sauntered into pews wearing low-rise jeans and thongs, and I would become distracted with unheavenly thoughts. I had never before noticed the level of dispassion in church because I never really cared enough myself.

The Doctors of the Church were serious, saintly men and women. I sought the quiet reverence of their type of worship, contemplative worship, but I became disheartened when I realized I was forming myself in a faith that barely seemed to exist. Though most Catholics proudly proclaim adherence to orthodoxy, largely on account of their position on moral issues, they fail to realize that even recent, twentieth century theologians would identify them as orthodox modernists. As difficult as it was to be Catholic in the modern world, and as much as I sought like-minded peers, I found little refuge in the companionship of other Catholics for this reason. I bounced from parish to parish looking for an example of even modestly reverent worship—proper attire, proper conduct, and proper humility in the sight of God—but I found not one. Some people look down upon "church-hopping" because abandoning one's parish does not contribute to its betterment, and it is a valid objection. But I was too impressionable, too fragile, and too nomadic to act like the parish godfather. I just wanted someone to follow.

My frustration ended one Saturday evening when I discovered a little hub of solemnity. It was a Filipino parish anchored

by a legion of tough, old matriarchs and their otherworldly devotion to the sacraments. They wore dresses and head veils, and
though not one woman topped 5'3", their demeanor set the tone
that nothing short of total reverence and devotion to the Lord
would be tolerated on their watch. They prayed before Mass and
after Mass, and I would later discover that some would visit the
church in the middle of the night and pray then, too. In fact,
for thirty-five consecutive years, not an hour had passed in the
parish without at least one person praying to God in front of the
tabernacle—twenty-four hours a day, seven days a week. They
set a pious example, and most every other parishioner followed
their lead.

My first Mass at the Filipino church was not life-changing,
but it was substantive. I was unaccustomed to the silence and the
intense focus on the sacrifice. My mind wandered and returned,
wandered and returned, while the small group of fifty parishioners seemed unfazed by any outside distraction. My attempts to
talk to God seemed silly and childlike, and I found myself insert-
ing *thee*s and *thou*s into my mental jabber like I was a medieval
hermit. But I recognized that my desire to connect to God in an
ethereal way would require noiselessness and attention, and I
new that I had found the appropriate place for it.

I began to attend daily Mass in the evening after work, and
with fewer parishioners during the week, the silence became even
more noticeable. To an outside observer, the sight of ten grizzled
Asian women and me must have been a comical paradox, but I
felt more at peace in that church than anywhere I'd ever been.
Within several weeks, I would become addicted to the quiet, and
it was a healthy addiction. I knew that I was being called to something beyond myself, and I felt alone but not lonely. As I entered
the church each day, the swell of every anxious thought would

abruptly vanish into stillness. I absorbed the stillness. The church would often radiate with the setting of the sun, and the second hand of my watch would urge the evening forward one millimeter at a time—past, present, and future tumbling over each other in quick, perpetual succession. I began to see the stupidity of my prolonged childhood through the lens of wisdom, and my future through an enlightened simplicity. I felt the joyful peace of knowing I had returned home as a prodigal son.

Most guys would call my metamorphosis radical and freaky, because like good automatons many of them march safely to the drumbeat of General Howard Stern and the minions on Spike TV and elsewhere. They fail to realize that the truly Christian way of life is anything but a soft decision, especially in this day and age, and having an identity with a logical basis is much more masculine than choosing not to think at all. Of all the challenges I have ever confronted—physical, mental, or otherwise—adhering to my faith was the manliest and most difficult.

—

MY TIME IN THAT PARISH was ultimately short-lived. For several months, I had been pressing for a new position in global marketing at the company headquarters in Dallas, and I soon got my wish. This new position would require significant travel, but it offered a less fast-paced, all-consuming time commitment during my intervals at home, so I moved once again—this time for good. My relocation back to Texas did nothing to impede my spiritual development. In fact, it intensified it. As I began traveling all over the world, the mental isolation that comes with detachment was enhanced through a certain physical isolation. I spent a lot of time alone, and I read more than I ever had.

During one of my first international trips, to Italy, a haunting image would become permanently etched in mind. I had taken a day off for sightseeing in Milan, and spent some time visiting the city's Duomo, a magnificent fourteenth-century gothic cathedral that is so ornate I could only visually digest it in pieces. Inside the church I paused at the memorial of a saint who appeared obscenely muscular—he was like Michelangelo's *David* on steroids. Thinking that this anatomically exceptional statue was a bit exaggerated, especially for a Christian, I peered closely at the nameplate to learn that it was the gruesome depiction of the flayed martyr St. Bartholomew wearing his own skin as a tunic. The shock was searing. It caused me to reflect on other victims of torment, like Sts. Stephen and Joan of Arc and Peter and George and Lucy and Perpetua and Felicitas and Sebastian and Thomas More and on and on and on, who suffered death through stoning, burning, crucifixion, crushing, decapitation, hanging, flaying, arrows, the rack, and my least favorite, being eaten alive by wild beasts. I found it difficult to grasp the type of supernatural religious zeal present in the hearts of these iconic figures, whose sacrifices were so foreign to everything I knew.

This type of martyrdom was not to be confused with the suicidal and fanatical kamikazes of World War II or Islamic jihadist warriors, whose idea of godly sacrifice is inspired not by love, but intense hatred. Rather, this martyrdom was the forced surrender of one's life at the hands of tortuous aggressors, all for God, for their own salvation, and for the salvation of others. I wondered at first if the brutal persecution of innocent people could be something pleasing to God, especially from his faithful followers, but soon I was forced to ask myself: how could it not be? Fundamentally, "laying down one's life for another" is the premier example of total sacrificial love—an example inspired by God Himself on the cross.

I reflected on whether I would have the inner resolve to offer up my life for God, especially through tortuous means. Perhaps I could muster the strength to donate a kidney to an ailing sibling, I thought, or sacrifice my life for my family, but could I really do it in defense of my faith? Though I had come so far, I knew that my quest for sainthood was barely underway. I was determined to educate myself further, determined to develop my prayer life and my passion for God. The more I knew about truth, the more I wished to know. Yet it was somewhat demoralizing that the interior conflict with myself, and my conflict with the world, increased with each new breakthrough. It was like a video game where every conquered level presents another challenge with even greater difficulty.

ten

mind over matter

AMERICAN AIRLINES FLIGHT 61 departed from Dallas for
Tokyo on a daily basis, and during my international
tour of customers and design centers, I was a frequent
flyer on the exhausting, fourteen-hour trip. For the globetrot-
ters who spent an inordinate amount of time on airplanes,
particularly the trans-Pacific Ocean hauls to Asia, developing
a customized strategy for comfort and survival was essential.
The ultimate prize, of course, was securing a frequent-flier up-
grade to business class, which separated a relaxing and enjoyable flight from a strictly manageable one. But when business
class was full and we were trapped in the coach cabin with the
other plebeians, we learned to escape the middle of the middle
row on the Boeing 777, especially those of us with thimble-sized
bladders. To beat jet lag, the "sleepers" calculated the best moment to take sleeping pills or throw back a glass of wine, so that
their bodies could best adapt to the new time zone. The "caffe-
ine junkies" packed large quantities of reading or watched the

movies they had missed in the theater, while the true warriors polished off business presentations and plowed through e-mail, or perfected their master plan to become the next Jack Welch.

My strategy involved a number of tactics, but I always had a difficult time sleeping, so mostly I just tried to read. Out of ignorance, I failed to pack any snacks on my first international trip, and my general distaste for airline dining led to the type of hunger I hadn't experienced since my high-school wrestling days. To add insult to injury, the smell of freshly baked chocolate chip cookies from first class permeated the whole cabin and I couldn't stop dreaming about Mrs. Fields. But after my first hard lesson in privation, I began loading up a transcontinental snack pack, and prior to departure, as a preemptive assault on hunger, I would routinely stop at the TGI Fridays in DFW airport to get in a good gut stuffing.

Early one Sunday afternoon about an hour before boarding, I took a seat at the bar and pulled out some reading material while waiting for my order of quesadillas, a salad, and a chicken sandwich. I brought three books with me: Fulton J. Sheen's *On Being Human*, *The Imitation of Christ* by Thomas A Kempis, and *Introduction to the Devout Life* by St. Francis de Sales. I opened Sheen's book, a collection of concise essays from the Emmy-award winning archbishop, and after thumbing through a diverse set of topics, I lost myself in a chapter appropriately titled "Education for Life":

> Man has an infinite capacity for life, truth, love, and beauty; he alone, of all creatures on this earth, has the possibilities of attuning himself to the Infinite. Since he craves the perfect, and desires to be attuned to the highest, it follows that only an infinite God can satisfy him. . . . Education cannot be understood apart from the plastic nature of man. Tak-

ing due cognizance of it, one might say that the purpose of all education is to establish contact with the totality of our environment with a view to understanding the full meaning and purpose of life . . . There is not a difference in degree between modern education and traditional education, but rather a difference in kind. The difference between the two is the difference between education and instruction. Education means drawing something out, as the Latin root itself signifies. Instruction seems to mean putting something in. With the passing of ti—

"Hey Linda, would you mind turning that up a bit?" asked the burly guy sitting next to me, referring to the television. He wore a dark green Eagles home jersey, which led me to believe he was from Philly, and his comment diverted my attention to the television.

"And next up on *Headline News!*"

Female Anchor: It's Oscar time again and that means the stars will be dressed to impress. We'll go out to L.A. where one nominated actress will walk us through the process of selecting a red carpet outfit.

Male Anchor: What did you do for Valentine's Day? We'll check in with Joe Bradizza who reports on the great effort that one Illinois lover made for his soul mate.

Female Anchor, in a deeper tone: And we'll head out to Baghdad, where a recent wave of bombings has U.S. and Iraqi forces scrambling for a solution to curb rising violence.

The news momentarily captured my attention, but as it faded into commercial, I faded back into my essays:

... he who concentrates too much on the succession of letters in a word is apt to miss its meaning. He who knows the world through the hourly commentator or the daily headline is apt to miss the deep current that underlies these events. The closer the hand is to the eye, the less the eye sees; mountains are seen best from the valleys, and the world is best understood when we stand apart from it. Otherwise our understanding of it is likely to become like an impressionist painting in which fascination lies in segments instead of the whole. What is actually going on in the world today is what might be called fragmentation or a splitting of wholes, unities, or organisms ... Fragmentation appears in literature when stories do not end, they just stop ... Fragmentation appears in medicine, when doctors are made specialists instead of physicians, and when organs are treated instead of sick people ... But the fragmentation becomes more serious when the world, a nation, and a people become split up into tiny little loyalties that are permitted to hold precedence over the common good. It used to be that people lived in what might be called "community" .. But today the splitting and fragmentation has produced what might be called a "collectivity," or gro—

"Who gives a crap about what these people wear at the Oscars," remarked the guy from Philly, to no one in particular but presumably looking for a response from the bartender. After the commercial break the news had returned for several minutes, and up to that point I had managed to shut out the distractions until his comment. Sure enough, I found myself mildly interested in what makes a Valentino dress worth ten thousand dollars.

"Ten grand? You gotta be kiddin' me!" he exclaimed.

"Doesn't surprise me," remarked Linda, her arms crossed.

"They should give me the ten grand." It was like listening to Norm Peterson perched atop his local barstool. He seemed entirely uninhibited. I pulled myself away and retreated to Sheen for several more minutes.

> . . . the principal reading of the vast majority of people is the daily newspaper. This means that their thinking is to a great degree standardized, that their knowledge of the world is derived principally from one source, and that what has happened is of little importance, for nothing is as old as yesterday's newspap—

"Here you go, hon," interrupted Linda, as she handed me my quesadillas and salad. I finished off the paragraph, tucked the book away, and proceeded to destroy the rubbery, cheese-filled appetizer. My hands and mouth processed the food mechanically, somewhat free of my command, as though my body was on autopilot while my mind was still invested in less trivial occupations. It seemed like one of those times when I was watching my environment rather than living connected to it, perhaps because my surroundings clashed so dramatically with the tone of what I was reading. I felt like a National Geographic cameraman observing the activities of an endangered species while careful not to disturb the natural habitat. I felt like a stranger in otherwise familiar surroundings. My mind drifted off and I wondered what it is that truly holds meaning.

> *Male Anchor*: "As every die-hard baseball fan knows, spring training is upon us." My attention shifted. "Pitchers and catchers report to camp in one week, and we will review the major offseason signings, what that will do for your home team and your fantasy team."

"That's what I'm talking about!" shouted everyone's buddy. I still couldn't get a handle on him. I couldn't tell if he was a little loose upstairs or if he was just a bit uncultivated. I always get a little freaked out by people who are overly friendly. He ended up roping the guy next to him, Frank, into a baseball conversation, and in minutes they were involved in a lively and curse-laden debate about the upcoming baseball season. By the time the newscast mentioned the Phillies lackluster offseason pickups, a pulsating vein in his left temple appeared to be on the verge of fighting someone.

"We'd be better off bringing John Kruk out of retirement! I bet you a thousand dollars the guy could come back and still hit .250!!"

"Stop complaining. You've got Thome, it could be a lot worse," replied Frank. They continued their conversation for quite awhile, and as I waited for my entrée, I snuck in a few more pages of the book despite my waning concentration.

"Matter-of-fact, I'm catching the 1:30 back to Philly today, and then in three days I'm heading down to Clearwater for a week to meet up with a few buddies for our spring training trip. We've done it every year since college," explained Philly Guy, who by this point had informed Frank and Linda that his name was Sal.

"You a baseball fan?" he asked, interrupting me. He apparently didn't care that I was trying to read.

"Yeah, I'm a big Sox fan."

"Congrats, brother! You finally broke the curse."

"I've never slept better," I quipped.

"Schilling is unbelievable. We used to have him, ya know. Gave us a couple of great years in '97 and '98 . . . Ya know, the last time I was in Boston was 1985. I scored tickets to Game 2 of the Eastern Conference Finals, 76ers-Celtics. Boston won that game. I'll never forget it—106-98. The Garden was hotter than hell."

"Yeah, I miss the Garden."

"I'll tell you what. I've been a Philly sports fan my whole life, but I have to admit the greatest team that ever played was the 1986 Boston Celtics."

"You don't sound like any Philly fan I know."

"Believe me, I hated 'em. But they were great; I'll admit that. You guys had the Big Three, Walton, Ainge, DJ. . ."

"Carlisle, Sichting, Scott Wedman," I added, finishing his sentence. "Who else? Oh, Greg Kite. He had as many fouls as points."

"Great team."

"David Thirdkill and Sam Vincent were also on that team. They didn't play as much but they contributed," offered Frank.

"That's right. Wow, Thirdkill and Vincent. Damn, I forgot about those guys. You from Boston?" I asked, though he didn't seem to have much of an accent.

"Connecticut."

I packed the book away because, like it or not, I was now officially part of the conversation.

"What are your thoughts on the Sox this year?" he asked.

"I like 'em, but I just don't see a repeat in the future. I don't think the city could handle it." The World Series hadn't fully eradicated my Sox pessimism. After a couple of inflammatory comments about the Yankees' ALCS self destruction, we engaged in a friendly and subconscious cockfight to see who could fit the most statistics into one baseball discussion as a way for three sports-loving strangers to validate their credentials. This went on for about ten minutes until the news launched us into a debate over the Red Sox acquisition of Edgar Renteria.

"I'd rather have Jimmy Rollins than Renteria. Renteria is over-rated, especially at $40 million. The guy hits .287 with ten homers and seventy-two ribbies and he gets ten mil per year? It's crazy. Why didn't they just re-sign Cabrera?" I asked.

"I think it's a good signing. I think he'll flourish," replied Frank, ever the optimist.

"I'd rather have Rollins for my money. Solid player, great fielder. He was at .289/14/73 last year, and he costs us next to nothing," responded Sal.

"Yeah, but he's coming up on the last year of his contract. If you plan on keeping him, you're going to pay him Renteria money. That's just the nature of the beast. Younger guys will out-play the vets some of the time, but the established guys are the ones who get paid. It's business. You've gotta strike a balance by building a good core in the farm," explained Frank.

"Yeah, I agree with you, and I understand a free agent pickup like Renteria is going to cost you, and I'm fine with that. But ten million? C'mon. You could throw Hanley Ramirez out there for 162 games and not be much worse off, and at least he'd give you great speed at the bottom of the order," I countered.

"C'mon. Hanley is a nice player, I like him, but he's a year or two away. I'm not betting the cake on Ramirez just yet. We haven't even seen him do anything above AA ball. October, Yankee Stadium, no way. People were in love with Donnie Sadler in the mid-nineties too, and he didn't do anything in the majors," replied Frank.

"It's just an example. I don't buy the Renteria hype. His numbers aren't much different than Jack Wilson on the Pirates, and he's definitely not a clubhouse guy," I replied.

"We may have overpaid a little, but it's the market. He's a proven player, and he's a Gold Glover. He'll give us forty doubles off the monster, guaranteed. Ramirez wouldn't scratch .200 if you brought him up now."

"But he wouldn't hurt you in the field, and it seems like that was the whole purpose of this signing. Look, I'm not saying Ramirez is ready, I'm just saying they could've found a one year solution rather than locking in Renteria for four years."

"Well, we'll see," said Frank.

"Yeah, I hope for the best."

By the end of the discussion, I had polished off my chicken sandwich and squared the tab.

"Good chatting, fellas."

"Yeah, you too kid. Be safe," replied Sal.

"See you bud. Safe travels," replied Frank.

As I made my way over to the gate, I wrapped my mind intently around the upcoming baseball season. I reflected on the make-up of the Sox rotation without Pedro or Derek Lowe, and I worried that losing Dave Roberts to San Diego would kill the only good karma we've ever had. Eventually, my mind backtracked to the baseball conversation at the bar, and then backtracked further to what captivated my interest prior to the conversation, which ultimately led to a quandary of trying to reconcile my love of sports in light of Sheen's concepts for true education. My head was spinning. In the liberal arts creed of "knowing a little about everything and a lot about something," the something for me was professional and college sports. I had lived twenty-six years of my life as a daily devotee of anything and everything related to the subject, and there was nothing I knew more about. In Jeopardy, I steamrolled all of the sports categories, and in Trivial Pursuit you could be sure I was looking strictly for the green wedge. My year revolved around my favorite teams, and for the greater portion of my youth their importance exceeded simple entertainment value.

But Sheen would ask, what did all this knowledge and devotion profit me? It was of no benefit to my spiritual life—to a large degree, it was an impediment—and it distracted me from more serious matters. So what was the sum gain of all this activity? Objectively speaking, did it really offer much more than a good time? Some argue that sports is a necessity for the common good, that it draws families closer together and offers people hope when times are difficult. This may be partially true, but our fetish with sports seems to have grown into pseudo-religious worship, and we feed upon a catechesis of non-transferable information, which produces statistics junkies instead of thinkers. The heroes and gods of many young men are the gladiators of the arena, and we create shrines in our home to glorify them. Articles signed or touched by these national heroes have immense value, personally and in the marketplace. To top it off, the single most anticipated day of the year for most men is the Super Bowl. In the age of free education, haven't we evolved further along than the masses in the Roman Coliseum?

Nevertheless, I couldn't imagine myself eliminating sports as a hobby or as a form of healthy recreation, nor did I see that solution as being necessary. Overall, watching sports was a relatively harmless pastime, but reevaluating its priority became imperative to the restructuring of a properly ordered lifestyle. I have heard it said that the fruits of your life are dependent upon where you invest your time, and entertainment, like it or not, is an investment that yields minimal returns. Going out for a relaxing dinner on occasion is a nice luxury; dining out every night is financially imprudent. Time is valuable, and time invested in the NFL or the

NBA is cashed and spent without any hope of subsequent dividends. Such is the nature of recreation.

St. Francis de Sales admonishes this behavior in his classic *Introduction to the Devout Life*:

> Sports, banquets, parties, fine clothes, and comedies are all things that, considered in themselves, are by no means evil. They are indifferent acts and therefore they can be either good or bad. At the same time such things are always dangerous and to have an affection for them is still more dangerous. Hence, I hold that although it is licit to engage in sports, dance, wear fine clothes, attend harmless comedies, and enjoy banquets, to have a strong liking for such things is not only opposed to devotion but also extremely harmful and dangerous. It is not evil to do such things but it is evil to be attached to them . . . they usurp the place of worthwhile interests and hinder the sap of our soul from being used for good inclinations.

Of course, the statement "everything in moderation" might sum up the solution for an ESPN dependency, which would free one to pursue more serious activities, but it doesn't quite provide the antidote for all forms of entertainment. Even in moderation television, movies, magazines, and the Internet can be morally destructive, in the same way that a moderate supply of heroin or cocaine can be lethal. There is the issue of addiction, and then there is the issue of poisonous indoctrination.

While there is nothing inherently wrong with healthy amusement, especially content that is edifying and educational, my child-like attachment to it became its own type of worship, and I became another parishioner in our country's growing congregation of entertainment worshipers. My affection for it opened the door to infection, as the steady stream of popular programming was largely adulterated with vulgarity. My database of rap music with its crude lyrics was a notorious culprit. What is acceptable by worldly standards, even when exposed through genuine discernment to be utterly reprehensible, becomes painful to resist. For example, while I denounced the great moral tragedies of our time, such as abortion and divorce, I allowed myself to become desensitized to the nudity and rampant objectification of women through various forms of media. Though I may have vocalized my displeasure with this development, I nevertheless supported the movement by indulging in the entertainment that promotes it, as though my faith in some way granted me immunity from accountability. In the midst of this confusion, as I satiated my entertainment needs, my own values became subtly re-oriented. I'd consented to the volleys of impurity, thinking that I would be unassailable, only to find that my moral armor had been debilitated by the attack.

I am too young to know when television went from being a luxury to a necessity, but I assume it occurred shortly after TV became affordable for everyone. Today, much like any other addictive drug, people just cannot seem "to live without it." Though universally accepted as a value-add to humanity, it's most substantial contribution is perhaps summarized best as the gateway to superficiality. It is easy to become disheartened when you consider that women who know nothing about the embryonic stem cell debate hold deep-rooted opinions on everything from TomKat to Jennifer Aniston's wardrobe. The same men who devote hours to everyone from Jack Bauer to Matt Lauer are blithely indifferent to the growing threat of multi-national war. The consensus among the population is that if it is not entertaining, change the channel.

Some people argue that television is a valuable tool for communication and education, particularly for world news, but unfortunately the news stations aren't committed to performing an unbiased public service. Being cash cows for large media conglomerates, they are equally concerned with entertaining the viewer as they are with reporting the news. It is no mystery that ratings generate dollars, and dollars run the network. Nowadays, the lead story on the nightly news is much more likely to cover a celebrity or political scandal than governmental regulation, international politics, or corruption in the Federal Reserve.

Instead of expanding the depth of our knowledge and maturing as free thinkers, our minds are almost exclusively formed by the mighty religious gospel of anti-religious secularism that the Hollywood illuminati preach from the pulpit of the boob tube, presenting faith as nothing more than spiritual consolation for the galactically stupid. Having sound moral convictions simply doesn't jibe with their social philosophy, so the one who draws a line in the sand between right and wrong is pronounced a zealot or a bigot. In a spirit of fight or flight, most people will sell their souls to renounce these labels. We have been suckled on the intoxicating milk of network television and its related influences, and it has united the receiver to the giver whether we have wanted it to or not. As St. Francis de Sales says, "We become like the things we love. Love makes lovers equal."

The moment I left school I stopped learning. Sure, I studied all about the nuances of my industry, read the newspaper, picked up a refried best-seller every once in a while with a title like "Ten Ways to be a Gazillionaire" or "Ten Ways to be an Awesome You," but any further enthusiasm for the arts, literature, history, philosophy, theology, or science, got sucked into the black-hole of my mid-twenties. I stopped asking questions. I stopped thinking. When I was a child my fascination with the world fueled my curiosity. I would ask "Why is the sky blue?" or "Why is milk white?" or "Why does paper money have value?" I became a glutton for knowledge. I remember spending hours trying to answer the question: Who are "they"? My teachers would often employ the phrase, "They say this" and "They say that", as though "they" were the final authority on everything. It was as though I grew up as part of a strange, never-ending Orwellian nightmare.

As an adult, preoccupied with my career and with dating, among other things, I blindly conformed to what "they" said without bothering myself with questions. I never challenged "them." No one in my circle did. To make matters worse, I had already forgotten, through sheer complacency, much of my education. I couldn't remember the thirteen original colonies. I couldn't recount the events that led up to World War i, or the size of a hectare, or the formula to calculate interest rate. I couldn't even answer the question "Conjunction Junction, what's your function?"

As I tore myself away from entertainment, I began taking a nosedive back into academia. I enjoyed learning again. There was freedom in selecting my own curriculum for the first time in my life. I relearned history, studied philosophy and theology at length, and found answers to seemingly impossible questions. I studied scientific theory on everything from space to biology. I verified that it was possible, as Will Hunting declared, to get a $150,000 education "for a dollar fifty in late charges at the public library." I began to understand, to believe, and to change with the confidence of one who could justify his beliefs through education. It was an important development, because I knew that I would eventually be challenged.

—

I BOARDED FLIGHT 61 and pulled out an iPod and my book, seeking to take advantage of the opportunity for some quiet time. The iPod was a little misleading. Though I listened to some music during the long flight, it was never while reading. The headphones provided a conversation deterrent to whomever was sitting next to me, and though it may sound unfriendly, I simply preferred the privacy of being left alone. In the past, I've been trapped in discussions lasting for hours, feeling obliged to talk for the rest of the flight and to sharing the armrest. The experience reminded me of a long blind date. You eat dinner, watch a movie, chitchat, maybe a glass or two of wine . . . only on an airplane there's no exit strategy, and you might get stuck with a dude. The date always ends the same way—the exchange of business cards, the walk to baggage claim, the "have a nice life." It was all very weird, and I avoided it.

I was seated in 20A, in the exit row. I settled in and stretched my legs, hoping that my neighbor weighed less than two hundred pounds. Luckily, a semi-attractive businesswoman in her mid-thirties approached, giving me the smile-nod combo, which in the sign language of travelers means, "Hey, that's my seat, looks like we'll be sitting together for the next several hours so I hope you're not crazy." She seemed a bit uptight and fidgety, and she wore a pin stripe navy-blue suit, a bizarre outfit considering the distance of the flight. I noticed no wedding ring. After sending a few messages on her Blackberry prior to take-off, she browsed through *American Way* magazine before pulling out a hardcover copy of *The Old Man and Mr. Smith* by Peter Ustinov.

"It is now safe to turn on approved electronic devices," notified the loudspeaker robotically, about twenty minutes after take-off.

She immediately set aside the book and reached for her Dell D600 laptop, reviewing a PowerPoint presentation for a minute before beginning a movie, which at quick glance appeared to be, *Sideways*. She made it about halfway through the movie before she swallowed a couple of pills, unfolded her eye mask, and covered herself in the complementary red blanket. For three hours we remained fixed in our positions, and we both skipped the in-flight meal. Meanwhile, I was tearing through Sheen's book. I enjoyed the essay format and tap-danced from topic to topic in quick succession: . . . the sexual revolution . . . communism . . . contentment . . . the mystery of love . . . middle age . . . atheism . . . education . . . the atomic bomb . . . revolution . . . equality. .. the different educational training of men and women . . . birth control, etc.

"Can I get you anything to drink?" interrupted the stewardess.

"Uh, sure, I'll have some coffee. Black, please," I replied. Quiet solitude, a good book, and a hot cup of coffee . . . it is true that the best things in life are free. (Or in that case, $1500 round trip).

"And you, miss?" The commotion had caused my neighbor to unmask, and she sat up straight and adjusted herself.

"Yeah, do you have green tea?" she asked slowly and hoarsely.

"Sorry, we just have Lipton."

"Yeah, that's fine."

Clearly disoriented, she slowly reached for the tea and inadvertently placed the cup at the edge of her tray while doubling back for the sugar. And because gravity still works at thirty thousand feet, the hot water exploded all over her legs and onto my jeans. The ensuing pandemonium riled the other passengers, and as she panicked, I made a move to protect my coffee. Without delay a second stewardess with cat-like reflexes pounced on the problem, enabling everybody to get back to their business.

"Once again, I am so sorry," said my neighbor, soon after the stewardesses vanished.

"It's nothing. Really. Don't sweat it," I replied curtly, sensing that I was being drawn into a conversation.

"I'm Janice," she stated, offering me her hand.

"Hey Janice, I'm Tarek," I said, giving it a brief, one-pump shake.

"What is it?" she asked.

"Ta-a-a-r-e-h-k" I replied, elongating each syllable, as was customary for me during every introduction.

"How do you spell it?"

"T. A. R. E. K. It's kind of weird."

"No, it's nice. I like it. If your jeans are stained I'll give you money for a new pair."

"Seriously, Janice, it's nothing. I mean it. It's just water," I said. I was getting annoyed because she was overdoing it. "It's the first time they've been washed."

"Oh, really?"

"No, I'm just kidding. I probably shouldn't joke like that. You don't know my humor."

"That's fine."

I changed the subject. "Do you normally wear a business suit on fourteen hour flights?"

"Oh . . . long story," she said, looking down at her outfit before offering a succinct explanation. "I had a meeting this morning and didn't have time to change. I barely made the flight."

"On a Sunday?"

"It's the only opportunity we had. I was in town for only two days preparing for this trip to Japan," she explained.

"Yikes, that's pretty intense," I said. Strangely, I don't think I'd ever said the word "yikes" in my life until that moment. It was a feeble attempt at expressing emotion.

We spent the next couple of minutes discussing travel stories, what we did for a living, where we were from, where we went to school . . . the usual. She was born in Iowa, lived in Chicago, attended the University of Illinois, and worked for a consulting company. I responded in kind with a brief and uninspired rundown of my stats and credentials, and because the conversation was relatively vapid, I found myself waiting for an opportune moment to sneak my headphones back on until she began a long horror story about her last trip to Japan.

"Anything crazy ever happen to you overseas?" she asked, after we got a laugh about a sushi mishap.

"I once got a speeding ticket on the Autobahn," I revealed.

"No way!"

"Yeah, no joke. There are actually speed limits in some areas. I was on my way from Salzburg back to Munich, and I was late for a flight. I was going about 190 kilometers per hour."

"That's hilarious," she laughed. "I didn't think that was possible."

"At the time, I didn't either."

"What are you reading if you don't mind me asking?" she said.

Her question caught me off guard, and I was reticent about telling her. If I had been poring through a Grisham novel, or *GQ*, or the *New York Times*, I wouldn't have felt as freakish as I did at that moment. It was as though I had just been discovered in my cave of conservatism, so I tried to be as nondescript as possible in my response. "It's a collection of essays by Fulton J. Sheen."

"Interesting." She had clearly never heard of him.

"I saw you reading the Ustinov book," I volleyed, before she could ask a follow-up question. "How do you like it?"

"I love it. It's great. It's a farce about God and the devil," she explained. Her response was typical. I've discovered that books are like boxers. Every boxer seems to have a winning record, and most books seem to earn a response of pretty good to great.

After our chat an awkward silence ensued. As we each made a move to retreat to our pastimes, an old prayer card of mine, doubling as a bookmark, fell to the floor. She reached down to lend a hand and paused to read what it said.

"Oh, is this St. Christopher?" she asked confidently, handing the card over.

"No, I don't think so. What makes you say that?" I replied.

"Isn't he the saint of travelers, or something like that?" she asked. "I don't know. A guy I used to work with always traveled with this little medal of St. Christopher, so I just figured, ya know, because you were traveling . . ."

"I didn't know that. No, this is St. Louis de Montfort, I think. I can't remember where I got it, but I've had it a while and I just use it as a bookmark," I stated, flipping the card over to look at it.

"Is he the founder of St. Louis?" she asked, feigning interest since she brought up the topic.

"I have no idea. I don't think so. I think St. Louis was named after the French king, but don't quote me on that." It was funny; I had had that prayer card for years and never thought twice about the person who was on it. It was a little twist of irony. I could recite to her Wade Boggs' batting averages from 1985 to 1988, but I drew a blank on a man whose achievements make Boggs look childish.

"So, are you Catholic? Actually . . . don't answer that if I am being too nosy," she said, thinking better of her question after it spilled out.

"No, that's fine. Yeah, I'm Catholic. You?"

"Well, I was raised Catholic. I was baptized, confirmed, but it was never really my thing. That's not to say it's not good for some people, I was just never able to get into it."

"Are you anything?"

"I'm definitely spiritual. Like, I definitely believe there is something out there."

"What do you mean by 'spiritual'?"

"Just that there is a spiritual force or energy in the world, and that we can tap into it to find harmony, balance."

"Okay," I replied incredulously, proud of myself for withholding an immature remark.

"I'm a big fan of Don Miguel Ruiz," she explained.

"So Mr. Ruiz has all the answers?" I asked, with a tinge of sarcasm.

"I don't think any one person has all the answers. But I do find Toltec Tradition to be fascinating. It's a journey for everyone, ya know? I certainly don't think the Catholic Church has all the answers," she countered. "No offense or anything."

"None taken."

"Believe me, whatever you have, keep it. Hold onto it. If you have something that motivates you or gives you the answers you need, embrace it, as long as you're not hurting anyone," she said.

Whether she intended to or not, I found her comment a little patronizing.

"I think it's all good," she continued.

"I don't know," I replied, as a preamble to disagreement. "I don't think its all good. It's either true or it isn't. Why would someone want to believe in something that's BS? I have more pride than that, personally."

"Well, I guess I'll have to challenge you on that then. By the way, you do realize we have officially crossed into one of the three big no-nos: sex, politics, and religion."

"I think we'll survive," I said, becoming rather interested in the discussion.

"Well, okay, don't take this the wrong way, but do you honestly think praying to a dead guy makes a lot of sense? How do you rationalize that?"

"What is so illogical about it?" I replied matter-of-factly, thinking it would be easier to offer her a decent response if I could get her to articulate her objection.

"Well, how about the fact that they're dead, for one."

"Well, do you believe in an afterlife?" I asked.

"I'm leaning in that direction," she replied, allowing her eyes to break contact as she thought carefully about her answer.

"If you believe in an afterlife, like I do, you could make the argument that they are more alive than we are, right? The death of the flesh isn't the end of life, as far as I'm concerned."

"And you think they can hear you?" she said, cracking a little smile.

"Why not? If they are with God right now, I'm pretty sure they can do just about anything," I said. My responses were not of the theological sort, but they seemed rational to me once a few basics could be agreed upon.

"But why these particular people and not relatives or someone else?"

"I don't know if my relatives are in heaven."

"That's bleak."

"I hope they are, but I don't know for sure," I said, lightly shrugging my shoulders.

"And St. Louis . . . you know for sure he is in heaven even though you know nothing about him?"

"Ouch. Touche," I said, laughing. "You got me! If the Church says he's a saint, then I believe it."

"Just like a good altar boy!" she said playfully.

"It's no different than going to the hospital. Are you sure your doctor is a doctor, or are you putting your faith in the diploma hanging on the wall? Who says he is a doctor?"

"Okay, that's fair, but this just has an added creep factor, that's all."

"What does?"

"Carrying around cards of these people with prayers on them! Again, no offense. I just struggle to see the value of it." She wanted to call me crazy, but she was being polite.

"How is it any different than baseball cards?" I asked rhetorically. "Look at Mickey Mantle or Ted Williams. They're both dead, but people treat their memorabilia like relics. Ted Williams even has a tunnel named after him in Boston."

"I've never even heard of Ted Williams," she confessed.

"Blasphemy!"

"But c'mon, that's different than this."

"How do you figure?"

"People aren't asking for their prayers. At least they acknowledge that they're dead. It's like the Presidents. We can resurrect a monument to them out of respect for what they did while they were alive, but you don't see people today asking them for help with tuition payments," she said.

"Well, Ted Williams is actually frozen, so there's still hope," I replied, only half-joking. "But I understand your issue. Look at it this way. Is it really any different than asking your aunt to pray for you if you come down with cancer? Obviously you don't think your aunt can do anything about it, but you're hoping her prayers before God will help in some way. It's the same with the saints. If I pray to St. Louis de Montfort and ask him to help me out, I'm just hoping he will lob a couple of prayers on my behalf to God. He's a good candidate for it, because he's staring at the face of God right now, ya know? Is it really that crazy?" As I was speaking I realized that I had never once in my life prayed for the intercession of St. Louis de Montfort.

"But still, why not just pray to Jesus if you're going to pray?" she asked, playing Devil's Advocate.

"No one's stopping anyone from praying to Jesus, but we can always use a little extra leverage," I said, lightheartedly.

"Well then, like I said. I think it's great. I respect people's beliefs."

"Also, it helps having someone besides Jesus to relate to, ya know?" I continued, fleshing out my beliefs. "It can seem a little tough trying to measure up to God Incarnate. Whereas a guy like St. Augustine, let's say, who had a wild side before becoming one of the most important figures in Church history, seems somewhat more real, in a way. More like me."

"Yeah, that makes sense. I still don't know that I can relate, necessarily, but you've given me the best explanation I've heard about saints. Thank you. It's interesting."

"My explanation was awful," I said chuckling. "I need to learn more myself—there's so much I don't know." The conversation had reached the unmistakable moment for a shift in topic.

"What about you?" I inquired. "What is it about 'Toltec Tradition' that is so fascinating? Is that what you call your religion?"

"It's not a religion as much as it is a way of life. God, there is so much. . . . Just the whole idea of living with constant accessibility to the sources of love and of happiness, ya know?"

"Sure," I said, not really knowing how to respond. We were both adding the question "ya know?" to the end of our sentences, hoping to establish a connection, but neither of us really knew what the other was talking about.

"And it's not all I believe. I draw from a number of sources. I just believe there is a force in this universe that we can tap into that is so much bigger than we realize. I think all the world's religions try to tap into it, to reach out and access it. It's a force, just like the sun is the force of all life, ya know?"

"Interesting."

"Basically, it's total awareness of life, freedom from the restrictions we place on ourselves, which ultimately allows us to reach a higher plane. I think humanity is on the cusp of a new state of elevation, I really believe that. Where there are no wars, no more violence, no more hunger."

"Interesting."

"I'm being serious," she replied, sensing I wasn't buying it.

"I know you are."

"Well, to answer your question, that's basically it."

"Well, I guess it's my turn to play Devil's Advocate," I responded.

"Go for it."

"How do you know what you believe is true?" I asked.

"How do I know it's true?" she repeated. "I just know. When you start looking into this stuff, you discover some of the most amazing things."

"But you've got to admit, you are definitely in the minority here with the Toltec thing."

"I just think a lot of people aren't ready for it. We've lived so long without truly understanding the powers we possess. We are still evolving," she explained.

"But how can you prove what you believe is true?"

"Well, like I said earlier, it's a process. We learn pieces at a time. I don't think we're ever going to be able to uncover all truth. We just learn bits and pieces, and we take that and pass it along to future generations. But a lot of what I believe is consistent with the writings of ancient cultures, and I think we can learn a lot from that. People are just beginning to update it to fit it to our present-day understanding of the world. Does that make sense? "

"Honestly?" I replied, with a face as if to say I thought it was bogus.

"Well let me ask you the same question then. How do you know Catholicism is true? Aren't you putting your trust in the writings of ancient people? Explain to me how it is different, Tar-eek."

"Well, because fundamentally, the way I see it, truth isn't just a something—it's a someone, whole and inviolate."

"What do you mean by that?" she questioned, visibly confused.

"In other words, God possesses all truth within Himself. He is truth. There is no other truth beyond Him. That's how I know I possess the truth. We've met Him."

"But how do you really know? If you are referring to Jesus, how do you know he was God, or the Truth as you would say?"

"He said it."

"Yeah, but people say a lot of things," she responded.

"True, but they've never resurrected from the dead. That's the seal, as far as I'm concerned."

"Well, how do you know he resurrected from the dead? How do you know it's not just a story?" she asked.

"The evidence is overwhelming. But ultimately it just comes down to belief."

"See, I really have a hard time accepting that position. I think people will believe what they want to believe."

"Like the Toltec Tradition?"

"Yeah, but . . . it's different."

"How so?" I interrupted, without giving her a chance to finish. "How do you know these 'ancient cultures' weren't making up stories either? You can't live life without belief, Janice. Our entire perception of the world is based on the beliefs of other people. We're all connected that way. The real issue is *who* do you believe?"

Just as I had reached the climax of my mini-speech, the stewardess stopped by to offer refills on our drinks, and we both accepted.

"I don't know . . ." mumbled Janice, to herself, thinking of how to frame her next response, but I changed the subject slightly.

"Are you afraid of dying, Janice?"

"Ooh, morbid," she answered, while still fixing her tea. "No, not really. I try not to think too much about it. Do you know something about this flight I don't?"

"Nah. Just curious," I replied. "It just seems like our entire lives build up to that one moment. Every single one of us is preparing for it whether we realize it or not."

"Are you afraid of dying?" she asked.

"Definitely. I'm worried that I might go to hell. It really concerns me."

"Did you kill someone?"

"Just an old lady once, but she was small," I quipped.

"What makes you so afraid? That's really not any way to live."

"Isn't it the only way to live? For one, I can't imagine that there is nothing after death. It's illogical."

"I would tend to agree with that."

"And I can't imagine we all go to the same place. I just don't think Jack the Ripper and Mother Teresa are splitting Mai Thais in paradise right now," I said, giving the Hollywood treatment to heaven. "It doesn't make any sense. There's gotta be another place, and I just hope I don't go there."

"I'm sure if you're a good person you'll be fine."

"I'm not so sure we have that guarantee. And besides, what is a good person?" I asked.

"Depends on who you ask."

"That's the problem. Who do you ask?" I said, though I was really posing the question for her benefit, and with a playful smile added: "I guess that's why I'm reading books like this one from Sheen. Trying to figure it all out."

"Well, you know what they say: The more you read, the more you know."

"Whose 'they'?"

"I don't know," she replied. "Somebody. The experts."

"I'm pretty sure that quote is from Dr. Seuss," I said, smiling.

"Well, at least he's a doctor."

"Is he?"

"That's what they say," she replied, perhaps more annoyed by the banter than she let on. She grabbed a deep breath and released a forceful exhale. Her comment marked the end of religious conversation as the 777 lumbered stealthily through the long and uneventful night.

Over the course of the next seven hours, we shared a few disjointed thoughts about the in-flight movies, the uncomfortable seats, and the airline food, but mostly we remained fixed to our pastimes. The flight became a little awkward, really, but it gave me time to consider the conversations I had had since my arrival at the airport. I knew so much about sports, and I could've bantered with Frank and Sal long into the night, but in the religious discussion with Janice, I felt hesitant and inarticulate. I wanted to develop the skill of rhetoric, but I needed better mastery of the subject matter. I knew that nurturing and developing the questions I had today into mature, thoughtful conclusions would shape me into more of a man, and perhaps even witness to a few people along the way. Janice and I didn't walk to baggage claim together, and we didn't share a cab or exchange business cards. Our farewell was just as bland as our greeting, as we departed with a smile-nod into the Babel of confusion.

guerrilla in the midst

O N A FRIGID MARCH MORNING, my alarm clock interrupted a deep, deep sleep with an annoying, high-pitched
beat. It was 5:30 AM. Nearly every morning since leaving
college my alarm clock would announce the beginning of "my
time," the hours in the early AM prior to work when I would wake
up in order exercise at the gym. Over time I had convinced myself that this routine was paramount to a healthy and harmonious
lifestyle, and I took great satisfaction in prioritizing my day with
a focus on me instead of "the man." I became physically dedicated
to good health and had a military-like obedience to working
out. I maintained this practice even after cutting out most of
my other habits, but after moving to Texas I lost the benefit of a
convenient evening Mass, and the only manageable alternative
was to attend Mass at 6:30 AM before work, in place of the gym.
It was on this cold March morning that I planned to go for the
very first time. I immediately struck the snooze button.

I had always made the argument that my intense commitment
to fitness was praiseworthy and medically justifiable, chasing

Adonis every morning under the pretext of "good health." But to be honest, I didn't care much about low blood pressure or cholesterol, or even about feeling good; I was mostly just concerned with how I looked with my shirt off. I had a well-paying job and two college degrees, so I aggressively sculpted my body in order to add to the "bachelor resume." I labored to transform into what I believed was the perfect man, and my body was a big part of the package. There was a monstrous quality to the Frankenstein I worked so aggressively to create. My vanity masked itself under the cover of "health and wellness," and left unchecked it made every effort to warrant its subversive existence. Psychologists will say that by repeating something often enough, you will eventually believe it is true, and I was a true believer.

I cared so much about capturing the affections of women that I became like any other dog in the carnal chase for "prey." I did everything to separate myself from the pack. In college, I remember asking myself, what is the role of a woman in the life of a teenager? In my mid-twenties, the question remained equally relevant. An unmarried man, I was confronted with endless exhortations from the world regarding proper relations with the opposite sex. Over and over again, society portrayed women as a means to an end, sex objects whose purpose was to fulfill the physical desires of men. This modern man was a James Bond of sorts, pursuing sex with a variety of lovers, driving fast cars, and flaunting expensive designer suits. That's what women want, I concluded. They want Colin Farrell and George Clooney. But Western civilization throughout history had always depicted a real man to be the antithesis of this modern-day lothario. He was described as a provider and a protector, which is to say, of women and children. This is the man I wanted to be. The answer to the question of what role women play in the life of a man was of less immediate concern than the role we play in theirs. Our mothers, daughters, sisters, wives, girlfriends, cousins, and nieces, should be protected. I believed they should be protected from danger, from evil, and from our own perversion. But to an eighteen-year old guy, or even a twenty-five year old, that mission is the subject of fairytales. Real life isn't like that. Men have morphed into a degenerate version of Peter Pan, life-long kids forever in fear of growing up.

As I developed my spirituality, I understood and recognized all of it, but my natural tendencies would never just cease and desist politely. My passions were always in overdrive, always grinding against my conscience. From food and alcohol, to entertainment and lust, to laziness and pride, I was fending off temptations every second of the day. I had a vivid bank of past memories that taunted me to return to my old ways at every opportunity. St. Augustine describes this torture in *Confessions*: "The very toys of toys, and vanities of vanities, my ancient mistresses, still held me; they plucked my fleshly garment, and whispered softly, 'Dost thou cast us off? and from that moment shall we no more be with thee for ever?'"

The higher I ascended in holiness, the farther I fell when I sinned, and the more embarrassing and discouraging the whole process became. As much as I loved God with my heart, and as many inroads as I had made in my faith, I still struggled to free myself from my old desires, and at times I felt helpless to let go for fear of what a life of self-denial would become for me. St. Augustine writes: "I had grown used to pretending that the only reason why I had not yet turned my back on the world to serve you was that my perception of the truth was uncertain, but that excuse was no longer available to me, for by now it was certain. But I was still entangled by the earth and refused to enlist in your service, for the prospect of being freed from all these encumbrances frightened me as much as the encumbrances themselves." Despite my best efforts, it seemed too easy to slip back into my old habits, or to take a night off from the labor of being just. I hadn't fully prepared myself for the struggle.

Much of my problem lay not at the point of wrongdoing, but in the preparation. For example, though I had convinced myself that my early morning routine was vital for good health, in reality it was then that the chase began; it was then that I began forming my particular habits. It was hard to remain unattached to my desires for women when I was waking up every day with the sole intent of impressing them. To be sure, it wasn't my morning workouts that were disordered; it was the motivation that drove the workouts.

At 5:39 AM, the alarm clock sounded again, and I reluctantly sat up in bed despite my fatigue. The morning seemed more difficult than most, but it wasn't the effect of jet lag. In forcing myself up for a reason other than personal vainglory, my morning wake-up call became exponentially more difficult. My body revolted at the thought of playing second fiddle to my spiritual needs. As I lethargically rolled out of bed, I rubbed my eyes and released a lengthy yawn. My eyes peered downward, and my body groaned for additional rest. I couldn't help but wonder if this ostentatious spiritual display was really necessary. God is good, I told myself. Is this really necessary? As the city slept, the thought occurred to me that I might be overdoing it. Unlike physical exercise, the personal benefits of spiritual exercise were less immediately apparent. God is good, I repeated again. He doesn't want me to be tired. But I knew of others much older than I who made this morning ritual a daily practice. Then I thought about my death, and it compelled me to stand upright. I knew I had a debt to pay. The scene was a microcosm of my everyday struggle between my spiritual yearning and my physical burden. As Scupoli states in *The Spiritual Combat*, "The entire spiritual warfare consists in this: the rational faculty is placed between the divine will above it and the sensitive appetite below it, and is attacked from both sides."

I splashed hot water over my face as the steam gradually coated the bathroom mirror. Through the invigorating recharge, the thought occurred to me that this was a defining moment in my struggle for self-control. I was being baptized into manhood. The training ground remained the same, but the mission became entirely different. The decision amounted to more than simply whether or not to attend church in the morning; it became a broader resolution to conquer my body and my passions in order to establish permanent self-control. I was forcing a break with a cycle of failure. For much of my life I floundered under the excuse of "nobody's perfect," the liberating and over-used phrase that affords guys like me the freedom to pile up sins in a careless and unchecked way. Ironically, being perfect is precisely what we are called to be! "Be you therefore perfect, as also your heavenly Father is perfect," instructs Jesus. Though setbacks are to be expected, they are not to be accepted.

I shut off the water and I stood, arms leaning forward against the sink. The fatigue was overpowering, and every movement demanded particular concentration. I reassured myself that this was no longer about me, about what I wanted. This morning sacrifice was an offering for God, I told myself. I had heard it argued that God desires our happiness more than our sacrifice, but I came to understand that, more than anything, He desires our love. Just as greed is realized through money, and anger is realized through violence, love is realized through sacrifice. It is love that draws a mother to her crying infant in the middle of the night, and it is love that motivates a father to skip the big football game to attend his daughter's second-grade play. In return for sacrificial love a person naturally desires sacrificial love, and in that way love is directed outward rather than inward, becoming in itself a living entity which bonds a relationship through a free-flowing exchange of humility. When love is directed inward towards an individual, egotism then incites the adverse effect, acting as the acidic agent that erodes and separates two joined persons.

God's sacrificial love is infinite, and His infinite love is witnessed in the salvific event of the crucifixion. "Greater love than this no man hath, that a man lay down his life for his friends." Just as God expresses his love through sacrifice, I learned that He recognizes his children through their response to that sacrifice. "And why call you me, Lord, Lord; and do not the things which I say?" In the same way that a man's wife does not need roses, God does not need our filial sacrifices. Yet it is precisely in these sacrificial offerings that we measure our devotion, and join ourselves to God through the most perfect Christian testament of love.

My morning sacrifice for Christ, my small act of love, also doubled as an offering for my future wife. There came a point when it occurred to me that if marriage was my future calling, my future wife was presently alive somewhere. Though I had yet to meet her, I began to create with this minor act of self-denial a nuptial gift more valuable than any diamond ring. It became the first rose in a spiritual bouquet of sacrificial love, a gift of myself, where I committed to preparing for the role of husband and father as a fearless, countercultural man. In the past, when I had surrendered to loneliness, pursuing a quick fix for my emptiness through my thoughts or in my actions, it was, in effect, an act of adultery against my future spouse, regardless of the extent of the crime. But through sacrifice, I began to experience the first glint of manhood buried deep beneath the mud of my youth. I knew that deliverance and purification could only come through spiritual discipline. As Blessed Anne Catherine Emmerich said: "The purity of gold is increased under the hammer."

I carefully glided my razor over the contours of my face, and I burned myself with aftershave to stave off future irritation. I showered, changed, and methodically buttoned up my white dress shirt and fastened my tie. Though my stomach rumbled violently, I would force my hunger pains to wait patiently until after Mass, a miniscule sacrifice that, before long, would become a joyful pain. The hunger presented an opportunity to strengthen myself—my fortitude, my will power, and my devotion—and in the process I experienced a spiritual type of nourishment.

In the darkness of that morning, I envisioned myself standing before Christ on the Day of Judgment, vulnerably balanced on the threshold between heaven and hell where justice lies. My vision of heaven was not the cartoon land of angels and harps, nor was hell a Halloween party of bright red make-up and pitchforks. Rather, in hell, all the perverse human attachments so often presented in a gilded exterior of goodness were now unmasked in their empty deceitfulness, depriving souls of God forever through their own seditious attraction to them. The siren of the damned has never changed. "I will not serve!" say those who, like Adam and Eve, are drunk with the false promise that they can be like God. On the other hand, heaven presented ecstasy in simplicity, where God reveals himself as the Prince who wore pauper's clothes, the King who is servant to the poor, only now fully resplendent in the magnificence of the beatific vision. This is what the contemplation of my death punctuated for me, the eternal importance of a life lived in holiness. Belief alone is not sufficient, I reminded myself, for "the devils also believe." It is belief backed by action.

I stood up to reach for my jacket before pausing on my way out the door. I decided to first kneel in prayer, to thank God for my gifts and to request the strength to persevere in the fantasyland of artificial delights. I prayed for the courage to stand apart, for the wisdom to stay separated from the anesthetized beliefs of my past. "Wrong is wrong even if everybody is doing it, and right is right even if nobody is doing it," St. Augustine explains. I prayed for my friends, friends who I genuinely cared about, who in most ways were no different than me. I wondered if they saw the world as I saw it. How we act is not necessarily indicative of what we believe, and on the lazy river of temptation it's difficult to separate the blind followers from those who see but dive in anyway; some are floating, others paddling, but the destination is inevitably the same.

There was an honesty and a rawness in my prayers, and I spoke to God as I would speak to a friend. I prayed that my body would stop betraying me, that I would appreciate the food on my table, that I would never devalue my daily bread through gluttony or waste, that I wouldn't open the base, semi-pornographic e-mail chains that floated through my inbox. I prayed for those I knew addicted to porn, and most especially for the men and women involved in the porn industry. I prayed for my own purity and for chastity, and I prayed for every woman that I ever led into lust through my own selfishness. I prayed for an end to the vanity that aggravated my behavior. Finally, I said a prayer for my future wife, that God might console her in her troubles and enlighten her in her doubts, and for my future children, that they would live healthy and holy lives. I prayed as a husband and father would pray, and as I prayed, I began to question myself, shaking my head at the thought of how crazy my prayers must sound as they echoed meekly in our noisy world. Yet even in my doubt I grasped the full power of my words, how my life was becoming a series of confrontations as I battled against myself. As St. Dominic confirms, "A man who governs his passions is master of his world. We must either command them or be enslaved by them."

"Amen," I said purposefully at the conclusion of my prayers, and then for a few extra moments I remained in quiet solitude. This type of training was hard, I realized. Of all the areas of my life that I sought to correct, it was chastity, I thought to myself, which presented the thorniest obstacle. So great was the exploitation of women around me, that I'd become desensitized to the onslaught of nudity: the Hooter's ads and the *Maxim* covers, the Victoria's Secret commercials and the Shakira videos, the Miller Lite girls and Abercrombie & Fitch, and on and on. These brands weren't relegated to shady truck stops; they were intertwined within the very fabric of American culture. They defined our culture in many ways, and they revealed that feminism's long march to the freedom cry of "equality" had come at the price of dignity, modesty, motherhood, and virginity. Ordinary housewives sought breast implants, young teenage girls flaunted thongs above their low-rise jeans, and women everywhere embraced bikinis as "proper" swimwear, regardless of the fact that they represented nothing more than nylon underwear. G. K. Chesterton once said "Fallacies do not cease to be fallacies because they become fashions." I knew of only one way to be chaste in this explicit, sex-obsessed culture.

I put on my jacket and firmly clutched my briefcase. Conflict was to be expected, and I welcomed it. Though the strategy was simple, it wasn't easy: prayer and sacrifice. The real problem with the world wasn't the world's evils; it was me. "It's not that we don't have enough scoundrels to curse; it's that we don't have enough good men to curse them," writes Chesterton. I asked myself: Where are all the good men? Were they nestled safely at home writing pop ballads for their Christian rock band? Were they trapped at work paying off credit card debt from a Las Vegas weekend, or perched in front of the television watching *Monday Night Football*? The good men, I figured, lay in everyday shadows, guerilla warriors in combat with themselves and the devil, perpetually determined to reclaim supremacy through an uncomfortable, daily martyrdom. I headed to the door to do battle under the tattered banner of a Christian. My days as a hunter were ending as I set out to defend the hunted.

twelve

the tempest

AFTER ATTENDING DAILY MASS, I routinely drove to work in silence, turning off my radio as a small sacrifice to God during the twelve-minute morning commute. There are some who would say that God doesn't really care whether or not we listen to the radio, but it was a small victory just in choosing the opposite action of what I was inclined to do. God cares that we make sacrifices, and those sacrifices strengthened me in my every day battles. My ineffective dating life and my career were the primary catalysts of my fluctuating moods, but I learned to control my emotions through my relationship to God.

For the majority of us, it is our emotions—anger, lust, loneliness, jealousy, sadness, pride, etc.—that are the primary instigators of our actions. We disregard the anchors of our beliefs to drift with the ebb and flow of our emotional waves.

For motivational speakers, it's money in the bank, because they find everywhere a willing audience or a vulnerable soul in the market for an emotional pick-me-up. As a society, we are a group of malcontents being shepherded through the labyrinth of life by cheesy life coaches and televangelists offering enthusiastic Rah Rah speeches as mock religion. It's not our intellect they appeal to, but our feelings, and we ingest them like heroin for a bad headache. People like Tony Robbins promote inner balance with one-liners like "Emotion is the force of life!" while Joel Osteen decrees "You will never be happy unless you first think happy thoughts. Conversely, it's impossible to remain discouraged unless you first think discouraging thoughts!" A different way of saying this is, "The reason you are miserable is not because you cheated on your wife or because you are an alcoholic or because you struggle with sex addiction, it is because you don't think 'happy thoughts'." These quotable capsules are more poisonous than medicinal, because the advice is unmistakably regressive. Con artists rake in cash through the formula of forgiveness, and success is guaranteed because people don't want to hear about solutions - they want absolution. They seek out the prophet offering the magic fix for all troubles, or the assuredness that a disordered lifestyle is somehow okay. And when the medicine wears off, these same people will inevitably return to the hottest new fad to get short-term answers and a $25-ego boost. I kept my emotions in check a different way.

—

One muggy July morning, a horrific multi-car wreck involving a jack-knifed semi and three other vehicles brought traffic to a complete standstill on Central Expressway in Dallas. Fire engines, ambulances, and other public vehicles rushed to the scene, and snaked their way through the impromptu parking lot. Even the access roads were jammed. I broke from my routine and turned on the radio to check the latest traffic report, and I switched from station to station looking for traffic as I navigated my way through a few commercials, before involuntarily pausing for the tail end of "Don't Worry, Be Happy" just because I had to. I breezed through a few more stations as helicopters crisscrossed overhead, but I couldn't track down anyone discussing the accident—not even on AM. It was mystifying. I decided to wait it out on a local morning show, where a game of Name That Tune befuddled every caller until some lady recognized that it wasn't Rick Springfield or Billy Joel or Phil Collins, of all people, who sings "She Wants to Dance with Me," but the never cool, party-favorite Rick Astley. *Come on people, this is easy*, I thought to myself. After an endless string of commercials and thirty tiresome minutes, I had moved no more than a hundred yards. I landed on a different station as a male caller forsook every last ounce of his manhood in one last-ditch effort to win back the affections of his soul mate. It was like listening to a cross between love show host Delilah and Jerry Springer, making it all the more insufferable. The conversation went something like this:

Host: So Brian, where are you calling from?

Brian: Uh . . . Tyler.

Host: Now how old are you?

Brian: Twenty-nine.

Host: Okay, what's got you blue out there in Tyler?

Brian: Hi Judy. My girlfriend broke up with me last night.

Host: Oh no!

Brian: And I want her to know that she means the world to me and that I would die for her. Without her I just . . . I'm just not the same. I can't explain it.

Host: Well, I think we've all been in your position before, Brian. At least I know I've been. Can you tell us what happened, hon?

Brian: Sure. I've been dating Sarah for three weeks and everything was going great. It was perfect. I've shared things with her I've never shared with anyone else in my life, and she did too. We've spent almost every day and night together, nonstop. We've already met each other's families and everything.

Host: Wow, did you say three weeks, Brian?! Hon, maybe things were just moving a little too quickly. Did you think about that? Just give her some space. Maybe she'll come back to her senses.

Brian: Well, what brought this on is, I kind of caught her kissing her ex-girlfriend out at a bar. I got really upset and she got upset and we were both upset. Do you think that was wrong of me?

Host: Ouch! Wait, did you say girlfriend?

Brian: Yeah. She said she had gotten past that phase of her life, and I don't know if it was an accident or if something else happened. I don't know.

Host: Ouch! Okay, forget what I said. You need to move on, hon! She probably has mixed feelings about this arrangement. She's probably got some things to figure out.

Brian: I just don't think I can. She was perfect for me. She's the only one who has ever made me happy.

Host: Well Brian, I don't know what to tell ya. I really hope you find someone else like that, okay? Keep your head up.

I'm sure it will all be okay. Just give it time. What song would you like me to play?

Brian: Um, Judy, can you play "Endless Love" by Lionel Richie? It was our song.

Host: You got it, Brian. Comin' up. Be strong, hon, okay?

"My lo-o-o-ve . . . There's only you in my life . . . the only thing that's bright . . ."

As Lionel crooned, I pictured an unshaved Brian loafing on the couch with a half-eaten box of Wheat Thins and a can of Schlitz. Poor bastard, I thought. No one likes getting herky-jerked in romance, even if he set himself up for it.

His experience brought to mind my twentieth birthday, when my dream girl of the moment, who I had dated for a few blissful weeks, popped into my dorm to deliver a birthday gift, only to unleash the nails on the chalkboard, "it's not you, it's me" speech. (As dump speeches go, I am continually amazed by how resilient that one is. You would think people would come up with something a little more creative, like how no one pulls the Greg Brady yawn-stretch-arm around the girl move anymore because it's become comically blacklisted.) As a minor victory, I had done some recon work with a few of her cronies, so I remained stoic and strong as she reared for the cold-blooded stomach punch. "No worries," I said, deflecting the volley. "Nice knowing you." The sting of that break-up was unduly painful because my six-month pursuit of her had intensified my infatuation. As I naively floated on cloud nine from one date to the next, the height of the inevitable fall loomed precipitously. That one single moment in my life's catalog of Single Moments is notorious for planting an iron-willed chip on my shoulder labeled "rejection." It would become only the first of many, but it was undoubtedly the heaviest. From that point forward, lurking in my subconscious, my lovelorn pride was hell bent on redemption, determined to transform my status into the 'one that slipped away.' Its impact on my overall desire for material prosperity cannot be understated.

By age twenty-six, I had never been engaged in a serious, quasi-marriage relationship like most other college-bred twenty-somethings. I was rather proud of that fact, though it was a dubious achievement given that I was by no means unfamiliar to the company of women. Dating had become the source of erratic highs and lows, and my erratic responses to those highs and lows created erratic emotional spells. I was hooked on the idea that ecstasy was concealed in the heart of a woman, and as a result, whenever my dating life was in shambles, my life felt like it was in shambles. One woman after another became a rollercoaster of letdown in an endless parade of too boring, too slutty, too flighty, too coveted, too rude, too drunk, too superficial, and too much baggage. No woman is ever good enough when she needs to be everything.

When I flipped the script on my priorities, I felt like Indiana Jones in *Raiders of the Lost Ark*, when he gingerly replaces the golden idol in the Hall of Shadows with a bag of sand before all hell breaks loose. It was an unpredictable move, but I began to see my future wife as a partner on our path to eternity rather than a means to earthly happiness. The *I love you forever*s of this world are ephemeral. Rather than languishing in a romantic homeostasis, a true relationship presents two lovers shoulder-to-shoulder in support, encouragement, and in love, as they advance towards their twilight with anticipation rather than despondency. By making salvation our reason for being, a foundation of order and purpose is established which eclipses the flighty, freewheeling disposition of our emotions, and most of all, infuses the spark of urgency into our relationships.

As I began to recognize God as the source and summit of my desires, I was rewarded with peace of mind and the satisfaction of being tethered to someone permanent. I never stopped dating; I just no longer needed to date. The phrase "love God" can be very cliché and so entirely vague that it is often misused, but the ineffable joy that springs from a deep affection for God can not be communicated effectively. It may be easy for some to rationalize God, or acknowledge God, or believe in God, but rarely do we allow ourselves to unequivocally love God. Some psychologists argue that the idea of God is a response to our emotional needs, but this presumption is backwards. Our emotional fluctuations are a psychological response to our lack of love for God. If God is everything, what else could we possibly want?

When God possesses your soul in a palpable way, it doesn't matter if the girl of the moment won't return a phone call, or a prima donna steals the promotion. The disappointment stings but it doesn't cripple. If, heaven forbid, a family member dies, or a child, or a mother, or spouse, the scar will linger forever, but it doesn't affect our reason for living. I trained myself to realize that nothing in the world should preempt our relationship to God. He is the one love that is constant, the one love that is endless, and the one love we cannot afford to lose. If I suffered, I became all the more vigilant. As Chesterton wrote: "Alone of all creeds, Christianity has added courage to the virtues of the Creator. For the only courage worth calling courage must necessarily mean that the soul passes a breaking point and does not break." I learned to be happy alone; I was satisfied. I viewed my existence to be a miracle unto itself, and all of my endeavors then merged in synergy of purpose towards the seam that unites life and death. I ultimately discovered that the end desire for my relationships was salvation.

—

NOT EVEN ONE MILE past the accident, as I accelerated the needle to post-geriatric pace, I was caught off-guard by a black Ford Thunderbird with a Kiss bumper sticker that swerved into my lane at break-neck speed. I narrowly escaped an accident of my own, and I thought about the driver of the big rig and his family. It was a bleak morning of extremes, and to add insult to injury, just as I hit the parking lot of the office a strained, choppy voice came on the radio: "Morning folks, this is Mike Walker with traffic. Steer clear of 75 if you're heading north this morning. There's a bi-i-i-i-ig accident to report. A jackknifed big rig between Royal Lane and Forest has traffic backed up a-a-a-l-l-l-l the way back to Lemon. Only one lane getting through, and looks like it'll be awhile before they get that cleared up. You'll want to find your way over to Greenville if you can . . ."

I double-timed it to the main doors and robotically swiped my company badge through the secure turnstile as other stragglers came rushing up. I hurried up the cement staircase, which was worn in the middle from wear and tear and untouched at the edges. The railing was a dull brown and pleaded for a fresh coat of paint. I proceeded along the main spine of cubicles before steering left at the print center where two engineers from my group waited for printouts of schematics.

"Morning, Tarek. Nice of you to join us," said one of the senior engineers joking about my tardiness, but not really joking. "You're just in time for lunch."

"I've been sitting in traffic all morning."

"Very original! You'd think a former sales guy would come up with something a little better than that," he replied, turning to the other engineer with a wry smile. He was trying to be funny, but it came out flat.

"I'm saving myself for the Haikus I'll be scribbling in my office while you guys are working," I replied, offering a little self-deprecating humor.

"Wouldn't surprise me. Company profits go straight to your hundred-dollar shirt and Versace tie," he replied. He meant the comment in jest, attempting to be "one of the guys," but his comment came out of left field and sounded more like an insult. Even the other engineer looked a little uncomfortable. To my discredit, I let the frustration of the morning get the best of me, and came back with an equally pointed remark.

"Listen, I just heard on the radio that Wrangler is doing a major recall of pleated jeans. Something about the Federal Government and crimes against humanity. You might want to look into that." Neither of them laughed, and I felt like a jerk as I walked away. It bugged my conscience all morning.

I veered right at the next corridor and marched another twenty feet, hung a left at the water fountain, weaved my way through a maintenance crew repairing a leak in the ceiling, made two quick rights and landed on the stretch run to my office. It was 9:15 AM. My office was uncluttered and relatively bare. Had it not been for a poster of Neuschwanstein Castle in Germany and a couple of family pictures, someone might have mistaken it for a guest office. I rested my briefcase on the desk in the same manner I always do, and exhaled as I started up my computer. Before even getting the chance to log in, Rob Jackson, a tall, well-built ex-lacrosse player from the University of Michigan, who was a longtime friend and colleague, whipped into my office.

"Yo, T, where you been, bro? Did you read Kirkland's e-mail?!" asked Rob, referring to our boss's boss's boss.

"Good morning to you too!"

"Whatever."

"Did you hit that accident this morning, man?" I asked.

"No, I worked out this morning," he said.

"I haven't even looked at my inbox yet," I replied. "What did he say? Have you grabbed coffee?"

"Just about to. Walk with me," he ordered, and motioned for me to step out of the office. I reached into my change drawer and rescued some quarters from a mass of pennies and nickels, and we headed out.

"Alright, hit me," I said.

"So first of all, you're not even going to believe who the new product manager is in Taiwan," he began.

"Uh-oh."

"Take a guess," he commanded, with a tone implying I wouldn't get it right.

"Tommy Chu?"

"You wish!"

"Lin?"

"Worse!"

"Who?"

"You're not going to believe it," said Rob. "Crazy Sonny Tsu!"

"Get outta town!"

"Mr. Sonny 'I can't speak a lick of English and I can't close a deal if my life depended on it' Tsu!"

"Wow. I'm speechless. I wonder how they settled on him."

"I'll tell you how they settled on him. Ching wants a "yes sir" man, plain and simple. Chu is too smart, too driven, too successful to promote. Ching is worried about his job. He doesn't want someone around who is going to outshine him."

"That is such a tragedy. We're gonna have our hands full," I replied.

"I don't even want to think about it!"

"Tough way to start the morning, mon frere," I said, as we reached the inlet to the cafeteria.

"Oh, it gets way worse. I'll finish in a second," he said, as he grabbed a tall cardboard cup. The cafeteria was abuzz with the morning rush, as talk of the accident, the earnings report, and a variety of business issues echoed throughout the tin room.

"Damn, I wish they'd get us some decent coffee in here. This is acid water!" announced Rob.

"Wow, you're fired up today, buddy. Need some prozac?"

"This is poison!"

"And I will STRIKE down upon thee with GREAT vengeance and FURIOUS angah those who would attempt to poison and destroy my brothahs!" I said, mimicking the line from Jules in *Pulp Fiction*.

"Nice."

"Isn't this Starbucks?" I asked.

"Yeah, it sucks! I can barely get it down. It's a three-dollar cup of nastiness."

"I'd trade my laptop for some Dunkin' Donuts coffee right now. Nothing compares," I replied, as we waited in line to pay the cashier.

"So listen to this," he continued, "On top of Sonny 'I can't hold my liquor' Tsu, we're now in a hiring freeze all of a sudden! They pulled the req for the team."

"I thought they said last week we were interviewing people."

"They pulled the requisition," he restated bluntly.

"They really pulled it?" I asked again, in disbelief.

"Yup."

"Wow, I don't get that."

"It's company cost-cutting, bro. Everyone else craps the bed and we're the ones who suffer. We blow out our numbers, we grow revenue by $100 million, we increase market share by 4 percent, we expand the product line at freakin' record pace," he listed, making each point with a different finger on his right hand as he detailed his argument. "And now we're the ones getting the Enron treatment for some shoddy, second rate performance coming out of Houston or wherever. It's asinine."

"Man . . ."

"Honestly, I could probably deal with this if it wasn't for the slap-in-the-face 2-percent raises we all got in February! I'm gonna walk bro, I swear. I really mean in it this time. I can't take it anymore. This is ridiculous. I'm working sixty-, seventy-, eighty-hour weeks? For what? To work harder? So Dr. Kevorkian can pull the plug and cash the checks?" he said, referring to Kirkland.

"Were you expecting something else?" I asked indifferently.

"Of course I was expecting something else! I expect some kind of freakin' respect. Just once I want someone to say 'Hey, we really appreciate all you're doing and all the money you're bringing in, so here's a few nickels for the ol' piggy bank,' or 'Great job, Rob. Go grab yourself a nice dinner on the company card.' But do you think they ever say that? Never. Instead we get more bureaucracy and disrespect. Why even bother? I might as well surf the web all day. I think I will," he convinced himself.

"It doesn't work that way. You of all people should know that. Welcome to the collective," I said. "You're another bee in the hive."

"I just need to vent to somebody."

"Alright," I said, as though he hadn't already vented enough.

"Dude, sympathize with me here. Why aren't you feelin' my pain?" he asked, taking the guest seat in my office as we returned.

"I feel it," I reassured him, attending to a few papers in my briefcase. "I feel it."

"What happened to the old T-Saab?"

"Nothing, man, I guess I'm just getting used to it. It's the same old song and dance," I shrugged. "It's funny to me."

"Getting used to it? This coming from the guy who blasted an e-mail to the entire department about how we were 'Proceeding on a slow death march to irrelevancy'?" he said laughing. "That still kills me!"

"I was just a pup then, Robbie. I'm getting older," I smiled.

"T, it was six months ago!"

"Look, work is work, man. It's gonna be the same routine anywhere you go. I'm learning to accept it. Middle-aged managers who are died-in-the-wool morons; long-term strategic goals that change every three months whenever someone new comes in; some dude who slips on a banana peel in the Caf and gets a half-mil settlement. It's the same everywhere. Just be thankful you don't work for the government. It's ten times worse."

"I can't believe what I'm hearing. T-Saab, are you in there?" he asked, eyes wide open.

"Bro, honestly, we've been at this for five years. We just gotta put it in perspective. Who are we to be complaining? Seriously. I got four Mexican guys tearing up my lawn right now for ten bucks an hour in a hundred-degree heat. Meanwhile I'm sitting in the AC drinking coffee and lookin' pretty, about to plan my next trip to freakin' Milan on the company dime and pullin' down a very healthy living. What do I have to be complaining about? In the big picture, it ain't nothin'," I said, adding a little Bogart to the last half-sentence.

"I've seen it all now," he said, shaking his head. "T, I would have never pegged you for a lifer. Never in a million years. We might as well give you the twenty-year parking spot right now. You're hangin' it up on me!"

"I'm not saying I'll be here twenty years, Robbie. Who knows? Maybe I'll start my own business, or maybe I'll change professions," I said. "All I'm saying is I'm not going to let myself have a heart attack over it. I'm not going to allow it to affect my family or the things in life that actually mean something."

"Bro, what the hell are you talking about? You don't even have a family."

"Well, when I do. You know what I mean."

"You amaze me. What about trying to accomplish something? You might as well be dead!" he said in shock.

"It's the only way to be alive, man. If all you stress about is work, that's messed up. That's when you might as well be dead!"

"That's what I love about you, T," he replied, implying the exact opposite of what he said. "You can turn an ordinary discussion into something totally philosophical."

"Think about it Robbie. What really separates the Nobel Prize Winner from the serial killer the next tomb over? They're both just dust. What's the reward for achievement?" I asked, staying on the philosophical track.

"It's about legacy, about leaving your mark on the world. Doing something positive. Otherwise, you're just a waste of space, man."

"Agreed, but what good is all that to the dead guy? He's still dead. He can't share in that legacy," I said, attempting to make my point by debunking the idea that success is tied to some earthly metric. "The Grim Reaper is a communist, not a capitalist. He comes for everyone just the same in the end."

"So what's your point? What else do you want me to do? Sit in a cube the rest of my life, not try to do something?"

"Well, what do you want?"

"I want a lot of things," he said. "I want to live up to my potential, be an executive or CEO, make eight figures and retire on my yacht five years later and drink pina coladas with little pink umbrellas and not feel gay about it."

"That's very righteous of you."

"Well, think about all the good I could do, all the people I could help with a lot of money."

"Is that your motivation? To help people? If you're goal of becoming an executive is to help people, Robbie, more power to ya. I think that's a very noble intention," I said. "But I know you too well. You're not working your ass off to be a philanthropist."

"Of course not. I'll obviously still need to take care of my family and my future as well."

"On a yacht? You'll be sixty-five before you retire, livin' it up with your vodka and prune juice for about ten years before you croak," I laughed. "I can see the obituary now: *Robert James Jackson III, 75, of Dallas, Texas died Monday of a prune overdose on his fifty-foot yacht. Mr. Jackson was an avid donor to Harold, the Salvation Army Santa at the Kroger on Mockingbird, and he is survived by his thirty-year-old trophy wife, Bunny.*"

"You're an idiot," he replied, as we both laughed.

"So, what do you want, then?" he asked. "Are you going to quit and go feed the hungry in Africa?"

"It's not a bad idea, but I don't think it has to be that radical. It's the simple things, man," I said, lifting my cup for prop support. "Don't get me wrong. I want to do a good job. I take a lot of pride in my work here, in my name. I want to see us do well. But work is a means to an end, it's not the end."

"Yeah, but you shouldn't waste your talents, man."

"Wasting is a lot different than reprioritizing."

The funny thing about our conversation was that I would have argued on behalf of Robbie only one year earlier. I had distanced myself from myself. I was able to find fulfillment through work, but not at work. The distinction made all the difference. As Dr. Peter Chojnowski writes:

> Since man spends most of his days working, his entire existence becomes hollowed out, serving a purpose which is not of his own choosing nor in accord with his final end. In regard to the entire question of a "final end," if we are to consider Capitalism from a truly philosophical perspective, we must ask of it the most philosophical of questions. Why? What is the purpose for which all else is sacrificed, what is the purpose of continuous growth? Is it for growth's sake? With Capitalism, there is no "saturation point," no condition in which the masters of the system say that the continuous growth of corporate profits and the development of technological devices has ceased to serve the ultimate, or even the proximate, ends of mankind. Perhaps the most damning indictment of economic liberalism . . . is its inability to answer the question "Why?"

Through my love for God, I came to understand the adage that work is not always about loving what you do; it's about doing what you do with love. It changed everything about the way I approached my job, my household chores, volunteer work, or even helping a buddy move furniture. Sometimes you work for love of family, and sometimes it is for love of a friend or co-worker or even yourself, but ultimately all work finds its end in love of God. His glory is both the reason and the outcome, regardless of our situation. I ultimately discovered that the end desire for my career was salvation.

The struggles and doubts attached to my faith always accompanied the cycles of my emotions. It was easy to doubt God when I was depressed. Easy to doubt when I hated my job. Easy to doubt when pressures became too much to handle. C.S. Lewis examines this struggle in *Mere Christianity*:

> Now Faith . . . is the art of holding on to things your reason has once accepted, in spite of your changing moods. For moods will change, whatever view your reason takes. I know that by experience. Now that I am a Christian I do have moods in which the whole thing looks very improbable: but when I was an atheist I had moods in which Christianity looked terribly probable. This rebellion of your moods against your real self is going to come anyway. That is why Faith is such a necessary virtue: unless you teach your moods where they get off, you can never be either a sound Christian or even a sound atheist, but just a creature dithering to and fro, with its beliefs really dependent on the weather and the state of its digestion. Consequently one must train the habit of Faith.

Faith is a choice, not a matter of emotion. This gets twisted in the overly dramatic, slayed-by-the-spirit, fall-on-the-floor conversion stories. Our emotions do not bring us to God; it is God who steadies our emotions. I learned this, and experienced the freedom of it, by focusing all of my thoughts towards salvation.

thirteen

the beginning

THE INTERIOR CONFLICT between the secular world and the spiritual life has always been like two dance partners struggling to take the lead in an endless, violent tango. The dance never ends. I grappled each day with the challenge of maintaining my faith against an endless stream of temptation. There were days when I fell, but those days became fewer and far between, and in those moments, it was humility that strengthened my resolve. As Pius XII writes in *Humani Generis*: "For though, absolutely speaking, human reason by its own natural force and light can arrive at a true and certain knowledge of the one personal God, Who by His providence watches over and governs the world . . . still there are not a few obstacles to prevent reason from making efficient and fruitful use of its natural ability. The truths that have to do with God and the relations between God and men, completely surpass the sensible order and demand self-surrender and self-abnegation in order to be put into practice and to influence practical life."

185

The process of changing my life was a difficult one, but it occurred to me that it was during moments of interior reflection—praying, reading, volunteering, going on retreat—that I experienced my greatest joy and happiness. I recognized the value of these moments, how they somehow had the power to peel back the contaminated layers of my soul and tap into the core of what I truly longed for. Generally it was due to the simple act of stepping away from life for a time to gain some solitude and perspective. In *It's a Wonderful Life*, George Bailey is near suicide until an angel shows him what life would have been like had he never been born, and he develops a new awareness and appreciation for his life and becomes a changed, happier man. But I struggled to maintain a constant level of spirituality for any extended length of time.

With every confrontation in my mid-twenties, I fought with uncertainty and a blinding sense of indifferentism. The discord between my religious beliefs and my lifestyle resulted in a spiritual stalemate, and I languished over how to move forward in the most difficult areas of my life. It revealed itself in dating, where I found fault with every woman in pursuit of the "perfect" mate. Though I was unafraid of loving someone, I feared the *commitment* of love and its effect on my freedom. It revealed itself in my career, where I constantly dreamt of a different job or company, hoping that the next step would finally become my work sanctuary. And it revealed itself in my spirituality, where choosing to take firm action on my religious principles uncomfortably demanded that I discontinue my quest for entertainment and gratification. The Christian faith, it seemed, demanded an impossible dedication. My problem was not in the belief in God or His role in the universe; it was in *committing* to that belief. I realized in my case, in the words of G. K. Chesterton, that "the

Christian ideal [had] not been tried and found wanting; it [had] been found difficult and left untried."

I made every effort to fulfill people's expectations of me. My rugby buddies knew me a certain way, my customers thought of me in a different way, and my church friends witnessed another side. I attempted to throw people off course, to even misjudge me, thinking it more advantageous to live my life as a chameleon. The concern over my likeability was far more important to me than any Divine relationship, and I feared the bull rush of detractors so intensely that I played the part of matador, deceptively embracing the expectations of my acquaintances while remaining cunningly elusive.

Nevertheless, I wasn't prepared to abandon God entirely. I attempted to casually "fit" Him into my life while allowing my secular interests and my belief in Christ to co-exist peacefully apart from the inherent confliction. I labeled this duality "living out my faith in the world." Undoubtedly, this was not love at all, and certainly not an example of living my faith. Though I publicly proclaimed my Christianity, I only tepidly dipped my toe into the pool of ascetic life. I took a minimalist approach to worship, subconsciously hoping that God's infinite desire for love could be appeased by my simple declaration of belief. I knew that the greatest commandment was to love God with all my heart and soul, and to love my neighbor as myself, but *how* was I to express such love in our post-modern, post-Christian world? What is a successful life, I wondered?

Society is quick to stamp the term *success* to every business tycoon, Hall of Fame athlete, President, Rock Star, or other notable personality. I've heard it once said that life is a succession of goals met and unmet, and those who meet their goals, whatever those goals may be, are the truly successful. As a result, the thought of becoming great, immortalized in the annals of history, carries a significant attraction for the overachiever. But since we all meet the same fate, and since a dead man cannot admire his own name inscribed in the history book, what is the personal value? In the end, it becomes a religious question, whether our works on earth determine our eternal fate. To a Christian, true success is more profound than any earthly accomplishment. As St. Augustine writes: "Why persist in walking difficult and toilsome paths? There is no repose where you are seeking it. Search as you like, it is not where you are looking. You are seeking a happy life in the realm of death, and it will not be found there. How could life be happy where there is no life at all?"

The orchestration of my new life would become a painstaking project, one in which I would adopt a decidedly subdued temperament. I would learn that confronting my flaws all at once would be an unmanageable assignment, akin to mastering all the pieces of a musical arrangement simultaneously. Instead, I divided my approach into five distinct areas—the mental, spiritual, physical, emotional, and financial aspects of manhood. It was in these five areas that the process of correcting my vices would materialize, where I would welcome harmony and beauty, and where I would discover the very essence of manhood in my twenties.

The gift for my perseverance was not slight. Like Adam, God eventually presented a companion to accompany me on my journey. Early one morning during the hot Texas summer, I sat in my familiar pew at mass when the woman who was to become my wife entered quietly and gracefully into my life. From the moment I met her I felt the scars of my past painfully reopen in remorse for the wantonness of my youth. She weakened my nerve, yet strengthened the parts of me that were weak. My sins seemed to magnify her dignity and the boundless generosity of the One who sent her. She was not the turning point in my life, she arrived in the aftermath of the turning point, when I was able to appreciate the sublime nature of womanhood and my responsibility as a man to nurture and protect it.

The changes in my life would continue when the producers of *The Apprentice* invited me to California to be a finalist for their television show. Months earlier, having barely ever seen the show, I had interviewed on a whim at the open casting call being conducted at my company's headquarters. The Human Resources department sent out a company-wide e-mail offering to pay anyone's salary during filming if he or she was selected, so I figured the offer seemed too good not to check out. But as I made it through round after round of interviews, the prospect of entering the world of reality TV began to make me apprehensive. I knew how invasive the process would be, but I wasn't entirely sure what I was getting myself into. On the other hand, I envisioned all of the life-changing opportunities that would arise from becoming well known. Fame is a powerful tool, I figured, and so few use it for good.

As expected, the show forever changed the routine of my ordinary life. I went from selling products to *being* the product, and I received a first-hand lesson on Bono's declaration: "And its true we are immune, when fact is fiction and TV reality." I became an overnight celebrity. Naively, I once thought that a show's significance was self-contained within its allotted airtime, perhaps extending only a little further to water cooler talk and the tabloids. But as I quickly discovered, the Internet has exacerbated the addiction to fantasy. Newspaper editorials followed my weekly trials and genuinely analyzed my activity from a "business" perspective. Bloggers and chat room junkies spent months tearing apart my idiosyncrasies, hiding behind masks as they shamelessly turned my pictures into fodder for their pornographic fantasies. The absurdity reached its pinnacle at the checkout line of the local Kroger supermarket, where my picture decorated *TV Guide* and *Us Weekly*, and where I learned through the folks at Teen People that sixty-seven percent of women in New York City believe Orlando Bloom is better looking than me. I became a character in the real-life drama of make-believe, and I somehow *asked* for it.

To be sure, the erratic highs and lows of my character development on the series came as an unexpected surprise. Throughout each forty-two minute episode, the marketing of our personalities, from the perspective of entertainment, was nothing short of brilliant if not dramatized. The experience as a whole tested my convictions, as vanity kept taking the lead in my inner tango, but the trial was spiritually profitable, as I walked away from the process hardened and more resolute than ever to become a small voice in the wilderness.

I never struck a movie deal or my own reality series, nor did I ink any commercial endorsements. I never wanted to. My return to daily life was subdued, and instead, I leveraged my fifteen minutes of c-celebrity status into my own small company, and I began traveling all over the country speaking to audiences about my experiences in life and in business. Yet despite any material success resulting from the show, my quest for salvation has remained uninterrupted. The following words from Genesis are a solemn reminder of our finite situation: "In the sweat of thy face shalt thou eat bread till thou return to the earth, out of which thou wast taken: for dust thou art, and into dust thou shalt return."

John Henry Cardinal Newman, the namesake of numerous Catholic college centers throughout the country, articulates this reality in the following quote from one of his sermons: "We cannot bear to give ourselves up to thoughts of ease and comfort, of making money, settling well, or rising in the world. Surely with this thought before us, we cannot but feel that we are, what all Christians really are in the best estate, (nay rather would wish to be had they their will, if they be Christians in heart) pilgrims, watchers waiting for the morning, waiting for the light, eagerly straining our eyes for the first dawn of day."

Preparing our lives for death is the greatest investment we can ever make. It is by no means a morbid exercise in despair; on the contrary, there is no greater promise than a happiness that will never end. Any goal without salvation as its ultimate end is as pointless as trying to live forever on this earth. The stakes are high and, as Christ teaches, many fail to recognize it: "Enter ye in at the narrow gate: for wide is the gate, and broad is the way that leadeth to destruction, and many there are who go in thereat. How narrow is the gate, and strait is the way that leadeth to life: and few there are that find it."

I know that my journey is only yet beginning, but I am certain that, no matter how great the greatness, nor how rich the inheritance, nor how divine the beauty, to recognize that we are nothing—baby, that is the beginning of everything.

a note on the author

Best known for his appearance on season five of NBC's *The Apprentice,* **tarek saab** was born in the U.S. to a Lebanese father and an American mother and spent the first part of his childhood in war-torn Lebanon before his family relocated to New Bedford, Massachusetts. He went on to receive a liberal arts degree from Saint Anselm College and a BS in electrical engineering from The Catholic University of America.

After working in Global Marketing at Texas Instruments, Tarek co-founded Lionheart Apparel, a Christian-themed clothing company. Tarek is now a popular international speaker and columnist. He and his wife Kathryn live in Fort Worth, Texas with their daughter, Mariana. They do not own a television.

For more information about Tarek, please visit www.SaabStories.net.

This book was designed and set into type
by Mitchell S. Muncy,
with cover design by Jon Simpson, Canonball Creative.

The text face is Minion Multiple Master,
designed by Robert Slimbach
and issued in digital form by Adobe Systems,
Mountain View, California, in 1991.

The paper is acid-free and is of archival quality.